JAMES L. LUNDY

TEAMS

Together Each Achieves More Success

How to Develop
Peak Performance Teams
for World-Class Results

DARTNELL

4660 N. Ravenswood Ave.
Chicago, IL 60640
800.621.5463   800.441.7878 (in Canada)

DARTNELL is a publisher serving the world of business with books, manuals, newsletters, bulletins, and training materials for executives, managers, supervisors, salespeople, financial officials, human resource professionals, and office employees. In addition, Dartnell produces management and sales training films and audiocassettes, publishes many useful business forms, and offers many of its materials in languages other than English. Established in 1917, Dartnell serves the world's complete business community. For catalogs and product information write: THE DARTNELL CORPORATION, 4660 N Ravenswood Ave, Chicago, IL 60640-4595 U.S.A. Phone: (800) 621-5463. Or, DARTNELL TRAINING LIMITED, 125 High Holborn, London, England, WC1V 6QA. Phone: 011-44-071-404-1585.

This publication is designed to provide accurate and authoritative information in regard to the subject matter covered. It is sold with the understanding that the publisher is not engaged in rendering legal, accounting, or other professional service. If legal advice or other expert assistance is required, the services of a competent professional person should be sought.

From a Declaration of Principles jointly adopted by a Committee of the American Bar Association and a Committee of Publishers.

Published by
The Dartnell Corporation
4660 N Ravenswood Ave
Chicago, IL 60640-4595

© 1994 The Dartnell Corporation

ISBN 0-85013-228-2

Printed in the U.S.A. by the Dartnell Press
10 9 8 7 6 5 4

Dedication

*To little Dillon,
his loving parents,
and their
supportive "teammates."*

Acknowledgments

Before an author can document beneficial observations and understandings to share with others, he must enjoy—or at least benefit from—an incredible amount of learning from others. How does one approach the awesome task of crediting all who have contributed to one's growth and understanding? In my case, the approach is with a great sense of humility and appreciation.

As the years pass, I perceive myself as one whose role is to observe and summarize. In essence, I feel I have gravitated into the role of recorder for an incredible group of effective practitioners who demonstrate "excelteam" behavior.

Certainly my most basic, important, and lasting help came from my parents. They were not only loving and supportive members of our expansive family team, but they also focused extensively on helping members of our family understand the concept of process versus content and, perhaps more importantly, principle in the place of expedience.

Amidst the abundance of marvelous mentors and facilitators in our schools and colleges, I am convinced I was guided by more than my share of winners. Among all my wonderful teachers, one stands out from the others. He has been not only a great college teacher, but also a great leader, mentor, and friend. Surely, John MacKenzie at the University of Minnesota serves as a role model second to none.

The world of industry and commerce has seen few dynamic executives to match Joe Wilson, the man who converted the obscure Haloid Company into Xerox Corporation. During its most exciting and successful early years, he led the company as a strong entrepreneurial risk-taker. For those of us who worked with him, he was a principled, humanistic, process-oriented listener, mentor, leader, and friend. He also set an example as a socially responsible citizen who, as chief executive officer, guided Xerox into its posture as a progressive corporate citizen.

More recently I have enjoyed working with four pioneering practitioners of feedback training as used to enhance the field of management. Dr. Herman Gadon, the Director of Executive Programs at the University of California at San Diego, has been a caring mentor and associate. I have worked on a much more limited basis, but nevertheless with great respect, with Jim Bolt, President of Executive Development Associates, and Dr. Marshall Goldsmith, Director of Kielty, Goldsmith, & Boone. And when it comes to principled process-senstitive coaching and feedback on vital performance goal achievement, my colleague, Dick Murlowski, is one of the world's best.

I deeply appreciate the magnificent assistance and guidance of innumerable relatives, friends, and associates who have been so supportive during my own excursions into team membership, leadership, and this project. Thank you, each and all.

And now for the book itself, Wow! What a great first draft I thought I had! And how much better the final product is! What a great testimonial to teamwork this book has become!

I am grateful to Katherine Gross for patiently typing and retyping the numerous drafts of the manuscript, and for sharing her tactful insight and suggestions along the way.

Jan Frances, a real word master, provided invaluable editorial guidance on both macro and micro scales. I can't praise her contributions enough.

Jackie Bohan, an associate who also worked with me during the creation of *Lead, Follow or Get Out of the Way,* has offered guidance, market sensitivity, and supportiveness throughout the development of this project.

Finally, how lucky I have been to have the unwavering understanding, patience, and support of my wife, Lilli, during the challenging stages of the evolution and production of this team-built book. To Lilli, as she would say or write, thanks sooooo much!

Table of Contents

PREFACE ix

SECTION I
Considering the Game Plan: Understanding the Challenges

1. The Helen Greenway Story 3
2. Good People May Be Poor Team Players 7
3. Watches and Gears 11
4. Lawns and Weeds 15
5. Cheers for the Superstars! 21
6. The Blessings and Challenges of Team Member Differences 27
7. Our Basic Challenge: Individual Expedience 41
8. The Golden Rule and Poor Mr. Guillotin 49

SECTION II
Winning Plays and Strategies

9. Observations About Truths in Team Sports 55
10. How Teamwork Works 65
11. Teamwork Means Working Together— As in CO 75
12. Criteria for Evaluating Teamwork 79
13. Recruiting and Selecting Effective Team Players 85
14. Welcoming the New Member of the Squad 93
15. Delegating to Strengthen Teams and Improve Morale . . 99
16. Meetings as a Teamwork Tool 107

SECTION III
Reaching Championship Levels

17. How About Vendors and Customers on Your Team? . . . 115
18. What About the Batboy? 119
19. Using Commando Tactics with Special Teams 125
20. Justifying the Investment in Co-Involvement 131
21. Peak Performance Teams: What Secrets? 137

SECTION IV
Feedback: The Breakfast of Champions

22. Our Needs and Challenges for Feedback 151
23. How to Give and Receive Feedback Effectively 157
24. Feedback and Coaching for Conflict Resolution 167

SECTION V
Teamwork for Spectators and Others

25. Teamwork in the Family 177
26. Our Teamwork Opportunities as Citizens 187
27. The Really Big League—International Relations 195

SECTION VI
The Post-game Show

28. Ten Facilitating Perspectives 201
29. If You Believe in Teamwork 209

INDEX 213

Preface

Several years ago I coined two laws about communications in organizations. Law Number One was:

At whatever level you are in an organization, you tell your subordinates everything they need to know—but you wish your supervisor would keep you better informed!

Because of this truth, and the need for management throughout America to address its implications and impact, I wrote the best-selling book entitled, *Lead, Follow or Get Out of the Way.*

The second law about communications and teamwork in organizations relates to another challenge that is at least as significant as the challenge of the first law. This challenge is our almost universal need for better interdepartmental COmmunication, COordination, and COoperation or—TEAMWORK.

This second law states:

In whichever department you work, you and your departmental associates wish the people in the other departments would communicate, coordinate, and cooperate with you more!

You know better than I do how much room there is for improving teamwork within your own company. But we both know there is room. Look around you. Analyze what you see. Think about what has transpired so far today—or what happened yesterday, or the day before. Or, perhaps better yet, think of what tends to happen *every* day in your organization.

I'd bet most of your associates consider and make decisions daily without your knowledge, even though you

- might have some information that could have contributed to better decisions,
- will be expected to implement them, *or*
- will be impacted by the implementation of the decisions by others.

And, of course, you and I know this is true. We know that your associates tend to surprise you, sometimes criticize you, or occasionally engage in open conflict with you. If one of your associates is reading this book right now, could he or she be thinking about how *you* have excluded or surprised him or her during the decision-making process on matters of mutual concern?

How can we possibly hope to:

- establish optimal goals,
- clarify expectations and strategies,
- perform most effectively and efficiently,
- follow through to timely completions, *and*
- achieve success after success after success

if we don't become more effective in COmmunicating, COordinating, and COoperating? How, indeed, can groups of any size find the excellence for which they have been searching (and thus become "excelteams") without more effective interactions?

The fact is you and I and our associates—all of us—do not place a high-enough priority on COmmunicating, COordinating, and COoperating. In essence, almost all of us could, or *should,* raise our own levels of commitment to teamwork as we address our goals, strategies, priorities, procedures, resource allocations, time allocations, and follow-through.

Shouldn't we all do something to address this universal challenge? With that thought, this book should prove useful to you, your associates, and all others who could benefit from understanding that:

Together
Each
Achieves
More
Success!

Considering the Game Plan: Understanding The Challenges

Poor teamwork happens! It is a natural phenomenon. The natural tendencies of individuals and sub-groups to neglect the interests of others, complain about others, or yes, even have conflict with others will not go away. But these tendencies can be managed or controlled.

We benefit from people wanting to be innovative, wanting to excel, and wanting to succeed. But if we are not careful, good people may plunge ahead in ways that seem beneficial within their narrow scopes of interest, but that are potentially detrimental to more broad-based optimization. As an unknown poet has written:

We are building up or tearing down in everything we do.

Do we belong to the construction gang, or to the wrecking crew?

This section is dedicated to improving our understanding of teamwork challenges and will prepare us to look at ways to achieve *improved* teamwork later.

Chapter 1

The Helen Greenway Story

"Someone ought to do it, but why should I?" "Someone ought to do it, so why not I?" Between these two questions lie whole centuries of moral revolution.

Annie Besant

"**S**teve's department is swamped, and they're going to be working overtime this evening to catch up. Is it O.K. if I check with him about helping?"

Helen Greenway (my secretary and administrative assistant when I was president of a Xerox subsidiary) would approach me in this manner several times a week. And if it wasn't Steve she was willing to help, it would be Larry, Homer, Joe, or one of the three Bobs—the other key members of our management team. This spirit of teamwork became the norm throughout our organization and was one of the main factors that contributed to 400% growth in sales and profits in the four years under this team's guidance.

Besides being an outstanding team player, Helen was intelligent, dedicated, and dependable. She used good judgement. But her most distinguishing strength was her teamwork; she set an unparalleled example as a willing helper. Undoubtedly, this exceptional characteristic helped her become vice president in three different organizations.

For Helen, teamwork was as natural as breathing. She set an incredible example for reaching out to offer help, having a broad view of the organization's needs, and engendering a spirit of teamwork in others. She also was careful to *volunteer* to be helpful and not impose herself on others if they weren't receptive.

People who knew Helen recognized that her involvement with them was available with no down-side risk—she was trustworthy. They also knew that she would respond to their needs, showing empathy and understanding for the situation. She was never critical of the person or group she helped. And if she heard critical discussion, she worked to focus those involved toward a more positive side.

How wonderful our work environments would be if all our associates exhibited similarly cooperative and supportive behavior.

How about teamwork in your own organization? Could you and your associates have established your goals more effectively, clarified expectations and strategies, performed more efficiently, followed through more consistently, and achieved your goals more successfully—not just during a crisis, but again and again—if you had had better communication, coordination, and cooperation?

Certainly you and I have known other people who are good team participants. Each of us knows people who, recognizing that something needs to be done, say to themselves "Why *not* I?" as opposed to "Why should I?" But it is a rare person who consistently and enthusiastically will deal with whatever need may be seen in an organization.

Others we have known may be just as dedicated to the welfare and progress of the total group, but they are more likely to focus their attention and efforts on fulfilling just the obligations of their own realm of responsibility.

Helen's wonderfully generous nature is not the typical approach to operations. Groups and organizations of every kind face challenges in developing and maintaining truly effective teamwork. Before leaving the story of Helen Greenway, we can make one more observation: You don't need to be the team leader in order to make a great contribution as a team player! As Edward E. Hale has noted: "I am only one, but I am still one. I cannot do everything, but still I can do something. And because I cannot do everything, I will not refuse to do something I can do."

The following chapters are devoted to basics regarding teamwork, and reinforcing the key thoughts outlined below.

TEAMWORK
Seven Key Thoughts about Building Teamwork

1. Establishing good teamwork may require substantial effort.
2. To be maintained at a high level, effective teamwork must be a high priority and be given constant attention.
3. Good people won't automatically be good team players.
4. Since different people have different ideas and interests, the challenge is to seek widespread understanding, to reconcile or at least to coordinate differences, and to capitalize on the combined abilities of group resources.
5. Well-coordinated individuals can achieve results beyond the results obtainable by the individuals working alone. This is the synergistic aspect of teamwork.
6. People enjoy feeling good about the group they are in, as well as feeling good about themselves. This has been called dualism.
7. Teamwork, as so beautifully demonstrated by the Three Musketeers, is a matter of "All for one and one for all."

Chapter 2

Good People May Be Poor Team Players

*There is a big difference between
hard work and teamwork.*

Jim Lundy

In contrast to the Helen Greenway story, let's look at the actual case of another good person and dedicated worker whom we'll call George.

George is a phenomenal guy! He is dedicated and hard-working, perhaps (by some views) to a fault. He's the first to arrive in the morning, and the last to leave at night—fourteen-hour weekdays are more the norm than the exception for him. On Saturday, he may work as few as eight to ten hours, and he usually takes it easy on Sunday, working only six to eight hours.

George is respected for his dedicated hard work, long hours, and high level of competence. He is one of the most knowledgeable, analytic, and innovative managers in his company. He is extremely skillful at assessing situations, considering alternative approaches, and developing workable solutions.

Because of his dedication and long hours, George was shocked to learn that his associates did not consider him a very good team player. In fact, they considered him to be a terrible team player—and felt his narrow focus offset his strengths.

Yet George felt nobody else so clearly put the company first in his or her priorities—nobody!

Some of George's feedback was direct, but most of it was provided through a formalized peer feedback system that has evolved on a customized basis with our clients. Associates of the particpants fill out questionnaires to evaluate what they think each participant in the feedback program does particularly well and not so well. The simple questionnaire also asks for more specific information on how the subject's performance is viewed in the areas of planning, controlling, organizing, staffing, communicating, and leading, with very specific questions regarding such matters as teamwork.

George's image of excellence in controlling (following through, etc.), organizing, and staffing was tarnished by descriptions of him as uncommunicative and uninterested in the opinions of others. He was further described as not taking into consideration the needs and interests of other departments, protecting (i.e. not sharing) his staff talent, lacking respect for his associates, and not cooperating with other departments.

As George and I discussed this feedback, he kept coming back to his task orientation and tended to circumvent discussions regarding the processes he used to guide his department's efforts. When asked if he could recall the last time he got up from his overloaded desk to walk down the hall just to ask someone in another department, "How are you doing?" a long silence was broken by "I've *never* done that. Why?" Of course, it was no surprise that he had also never approached anybody else in the company to ask if he or his people could be of help.

George's excuse for tending his own fences was all-too-typical—he was too busy with his own set of challenges and crises to be so frivolous as to volunteer to help anyone else. And he understandably took comfort in that position.

By placing teamwork activities very low on his list of priorities, George was destined to initiate and create new demands on his time. Yet early input from others would have helped George achieve *better* initial results in *less* time and would have prevented George and his associates from wasting time later, trying to overcome problems and crises resulting from their uncoordinated efforts.

In a similar situation, a well-meaning president spent too much of his time traveling to visit customers—to the consternation of his staff and particularly to the displeasure of the vice president of sales and marketing. In his absence, the staff tried to fulfill their individual responsibilities. Even when he was in town, the president dealt with each worker individually. He never held staff meetings and almost never met with his key officers in a group setting. Further, in the absence of coordinative meetings, he had not established any substitute mechanism of communications (such as exchanging departmental progress reports).

The key executives in this company would probably, by most people's standards, have been viewed as capable individuals. Without coordination, however, they lacked a clear sense of the overall mission and they subsequently couldn't focus their efforts.

Unfortunately, the subordinates did not fill the coordinative vacuum created by their chief executive. As a result, the company floundered—good people exhibited increased stress and open conflict. Before the president was replaced, outright departmental warfare prevailed. There was even some question as to whether the company would be able to survive while recuperating from disjointed behaviors.

Fortunately, improved performance was achieved in both situations. George ventured down the hall, and his involvement with his associates became more productive. His results improved and his work week shrank. The uncoordinated management team was brought into focus by its new leader (who is a master in engendering productive team efforts) and the company is prospering.

These two stories relate to challenges in maintaining good lateral (interdepartmental) teamwork. Teamwork also involves the ability (or inability) of a supervisor to allow his or her subordinates to participate extensively on the *intra*departmental team. The challenge arises from outstanding people who, with great ability and a zest for excellence, are unwilling or unable to delegate effectively. The better the supervisor is as a *specialist* (as differentiated from as a leader), the more likely he or she is to be concerned about having this specialty done *right* by his or her department—and therefore, the more likely the supervisor is to do the work himself or herself. This challenge, and its remedies, are discussed in Chapter 15 on delegation.

Watches and Gears

*No one of us can be effective
as all of us.*
Unknown

As a youngster, I was fascinated by my cousin's skill at repairing watches. I frequently visited my uncle's jewelry store just to watch Paul delicately disassemble the watches one part at a time. The parts would be laid out in a straight line, in the order they were removed. To reassemble the watch, Paul would simply reverse the order, picking up the part furthest from the watch until he had put the last one in. It was a simple system, but it helped assure that the watch ultimately would return to its proper assembled state.

While the parts were lined up on the clean surface, I admired not only their individual beauty, but also their complexity and symmetry. However, while the parts were in a strewn-out configuration, the watch didn't keep very good time. In fact, it didn't keep time at all!

Teams can be likened to watches. If each individual shines alone, like a quality gear or spring in a watch, that's great. And in building a top-flight team, it is important that the person with the proper qualities be recruited to fill each position on that team. But like the watch, the team won't maximize its performance unless the elements are properly integrated.

Athletes in team sports learn about the importance of interdependence—and, generally, the best of them pay attention to it sooner rather than later. You can't be a great pitcher without help from a good catcher, and no matter how great you are as a pitcher, you won't win ball games unless your *team* outscores the opposition!

Those of us who play (or have played) in the backfields of football teams quickly learn the importance of the often-unsung linemen—and the learning process often is through the school of *truly* hard knocks!

One celebrity tells of his football days and of how he perhaps let everyone (including his teammates) know a little too clearly how good he thought he was as a back. During one game, his offensive line chose not to block for him at all on three consecutive plays, leaving him to be all but butchered by the defensive line. For those three plays the team was more like a disassembled watch—a lot of individual gears not functioning together as intended.

Before becoming a major league umpire, Chick Honachick was my baseball coach. Chick knew how to mold athletic teams. He was a principled decision-maker who handled each individual and each situation according to the team's best interest. Picture our team at bat in the last half of the ninth inning, one run behind, a runner on third, and one out. If Coach Honachick thought a squeeze bunt to tie the game—and hopefully win it—was best for the team, he would signal the batter accordingly. If the batter ignored the bunt signal and hit away hoping to be a game-winning hero, the coach would bench the batter in the next game even if he had homered and won the game for us! A lesser coach would have greeted the errant slugger at the plate, delighting in the victory, but ultimately jeopardizing the team's future as a cohesive group.

Coach Honachick, with his masterful dedication to developing teams that worked like smoothly running watches, had the best win-loss record among the coaches in the region. He knew that good players, like the beautiful parts of a watch, needed to interact properly to win. They shouldn't just shine individually like the disassembled gears of a timepiece.

Lou Holtz has established his reputation as an outstanding and principled football coach. Before a major game at USC in the late 1980s, two of his Notre Dame players were late for the team dinner—for the fourth time. They apparently had been touring and shopping, and hadn't bothered to get back on time. One was a valued member of the starting offensive team, and the other was a similarly key starter for the defense. Yet Holtz felt that *in the long run* his team would perform more effectively if he disciplined the two players—even at the possible expense of the next day's performance. So the players were sent back to South Bend before the game and the news wires hummed with the story. (Oh, by the way, Notre Dame, playing well as a team, won the game!)

John Wooden is almost certainly the most respected collegiate basketball coach of all time. His UCLA teams won 88 games in a row and ten national championships in 27 years. His teams also won 36 consecutive playoff games.

Wooden, like most good coaches, wanted his teams to do well on the basics consistently, and he wanted his players to be oriented to teamwork at all times. The basics as he focused on them were passing, dribbling, and shooting. And his definition of teamwork was to always consider passing before shooting!

While he was active as a pro, O.J. Simpson was a coach's dream. He worked hard on football basics and excelled at them. But he also constantly thought about teamwork, and always credited his teammates with their key contributions to his success. In fact, O.J. would delay post-game interviews until his teammates were around so they could share in the spotlight.

I have fond memories of a spirited athlete who was my teammate on several different varsity teams. Wally Olhoeft was a good athlete, but one of his major contributions to teamwork was his constant upbeat attitude. He was our built-in cheerleader. He looked forward to the opportunity to win, never backward to affix blame. When we got behind, his can-do spirit (as much as anything else) would rally us to success.

What a wonderful example he set! What an influence he was! What a shame there aren't more like him in all groups! Wally, like Helen Greenway, was great at helping the "gears" work smoothly together.

Chapter 4

Lawns and Weeds

*We will never be better as a team
than we are to each other.*

Unknown

If you have the finest lawn in the neighborhood—the one with a carpet of plush green grass which is virtually weed-free—you know two things for sure. First, it took a tremendous amount of work to establish that exceptional lawn, and second, constant attention is needed to maintain it. If you don't fertilize the lawn periodically, cut it weekly, and keep the weeds from maturing, the lawn will deteriorate rapidly. Like a fine lawn, teamwork is a challenge to establish and requires high-priority attention to maintain its quality.

It's natural for people to identify more closely with the small group than with the larger group encompassing the smaller entities. Members of a sales branch are likely to feel stronger bonds among themselves than with others at regional or headquarter offices. Production department employees will tend to identify with each other better than they identify with office staff or engineers and vice versa.

In hospitals, the doctors are likely to place more emphasis on their own interests than on the best interests of the organization as a whole. Similarly, the nurses will tend to view themselves as "we" and all others as "they"—as do the orderlies, volunteers, and administrators. It is even likely that third-floor nurses will differ with those on the second floor, and those on the day shift may focus on their interests counter, perhaps, to the interests of those on each of the night shifts.

This tendency has been labelled the "we-they" syndrome. One chief executive officer defines we-they this way: "we" includes *everyone* in the company and "they" are all others. He emphatically adds, "And don't let me ever hear these words used otherwise!" Such an edict is easier to voice than to achieve.

Other executives who opt for improved teamwork have broadened the definition. Strong teamwork advocates may want to include the company's vendors and customers as important members of their team—and strive accordingly to make principled decisions in the best long-term interests of this more comprehensive group.

The we-they syndrome manifests itself throughout society. Interschool rivalries and competition exist within cities, and intercity rivalries occur within states. In Washington, D.C., "pork-barreling" legislators pursue the specific "we" interests of their own districts or states. And where would our defense industries be if it weren't for the we-they issues between countries world-wide?

Our tendencies to focus on our own priorities or the priorities of our sub-unit (often at the expense of the organization as a whole) are the "weeds" that constantly threaten to spoil our teamwork "lawns." We have our own priorities—and they tend to be more in focus for our own jobs, responsibilities, problems, challenges, sub-units, sections, departments, or divisions than with the priorities of the total group.

Fostering fine teamwork lawns entails continual focus on goals to prevent the all-too-natural sprouting of weeds. As in the lawn, the seeds of anti-teamwork weeds are always present. When they germinate, they need to be addressed immediately—before the beautiful teamwork lawn is threatened any further. Managers often overlook the deterioration of teamwork until relationships have been strained to the utmost—or, so to speak, until the weeds have taken over.

We might classify our weed problems into four progressively serious groups:

1. germination of the weed seed: oversight or neglect
2. small weeds: territory or domain issues
3. medium weeds: complaints about or criticism of others
4. large weeds: choosing sides, open conflicts, or sabotage

First, let's examine the germination of the seeds. At this stage the malfunctioning of the organization is hardly visible. But through oversight or neglect, the deterioration of teamwork has begun. Several years ago, a hospital administrator and his facilities manager decided to postpone the completion of a new wing for six months. The dedicated personnel manager, however, was not notified for several weeks, during which he continued his full-blown recruitment campaign. Imagine the consequences. There were, of course, profuse apologies made to him along with the tardy message of "Oh, by the way, we forgot to tell you that . . ."

Similar weeds germinate any time one department or group decides something without input from the other departments that may be impacted (directly or indirectly) by the decision. Apologists may say they assumed what they did would be all right with you or that there wasn't enough time available to check with you before implementing the unilateral decision. But the fact remains, as in the case of the dedicated suboptimizer syndrome described in Chapter 6, *good people must be considerate as well as committed to be good teammates.*

Small weeds pop above the otherwise smooth lawn when someone says, "That's not my job," or, "You shouldn't be doing that because that activity belongs to *our* department." These attitudes might be referred to as "territory-itis" or "domain poisoning." In fact, it has been said that organizations can get sick—or even die—from domain poisoning!

The that's-not-my-job syndrome is so prevalent that many organization heads opt not to develop organization charts or job descriptions. Their logic is if there isn't a clear delineation of job duties, there can be no basis for anyone to say, "That's not my job." The price which typically is paid for this particular preventative medicine is that employees don't understand their duties, and they pursue ill-defined missions with performance gaps and performance overlaps.

When people complain about each other frequently, call each other names, or blame someone else for anything that isn't right, the weeds have grown to medium size. At this stage, comments such as these are frequent: "I wish those engineering geniuses would listen to us before they design these #*$% devices," or, "Why don't those paper-shufflers in the office get off our backs. Don't they know we have more important things to do than getting our expense reports in to meet some artificial deadline?"

There are other manifestations of medium weeds in our teamwork lawn. A manager may return from a monthly management meeting during which his or her department was asked to change or create something new for the good of the company. He or she is likely to introduce the subject to the others in the department with a phrase like, "Boy, you can't believe what they've done to us now!"

When open conflict, mutual harassment, and internal sabotage occur and persist (for whatever reason) in an organization, the teamwork lawn has all but disappeared. Managers in two different organizations commented that if they didn't retaliate in some way, "eventually they'll walk all over us!" *Retaliate?* Were they talking about our country if attacked by another? Our company against unfair practices by a competitor? Not at all! Both were talking about having *their department* retaliate against *another department* within the same organization!

Once I witnessed the calling of an emergency meeting of a department's key people. The urgency expressed by both the words and tone of the vice president's secretary is still vivid in my memory. As we hurriedly gathered, we were curious what customer crisis or great opportunity led to the special mid-afternoon meeting. What a shock it was when we learned the real reason!

This department head disliked one of the other department heads—they argued fairly often. The department head announced: "I'm going to get John if it's the last thing I do!" The meeting was devoted to details of his demand that mistakes of John's department be brought to his attention immediately and that no communication or cooperation with those in the other department occur without his prior approval. Clearly, war had been declared!

Unfortunately, executives like this aggressive department head often are described admiringly as dynamic or hard-charging—and often their feudal style goes unchallenged and uncorrected.

In another situation, a CEO began his monthly meeting by soliciting departmental reports from those sitting around the conference table. When it was the controller's turn to report, he said, "My report this month is in two parts. You already have the financials, and I'd be happy to discuss any questions you might have about them. In addition, I have here copies of a study we just completed on apparent expense report abuses on the part of many of our field salespeople."

As he started to pass the stack of copies around the table, he looked at the vice president of sales and added, "By the way, Sam, I'm sorry we couldn't get a copy to you in advance, but we just got them back from the printing department a few minutes ago." Amazingly, this was the first time Sam had heard that a study of his people had been undertaken.

Sadly, the CEO's apparent enjoyment of the excitement stemming from this kind of behavior exceeded the concern he had for building positive relationships and cooperation among his key associates. He allowed the reports to be passed out as the controller had intended. Wouldn't it have been better to suggest that the controller and Sam discuss the study results and ask that they involve the CEO later if they needed any help or decisions from him?

The cases described in this chapter illustrate deterioration in teamwork comparable to the cropping up of weeds in our otherwise fine lawns. When such deterioration occurs, it is up to the participants to address it so that the situation can be moved toward its ideal state—and hopefully kept there in the future. Suggestions for how to do so are the subjects of subsequent chapters.

Chapter 5

Cheers for the Superstars!

The world is moved not only by the mighty shoves of the heroes but also by the aggregate of the tiny pushes of each honest worker.

Helen Keller

In discussions on teamwork, the question about the need for *individual* ability and *individual* effort to ensure effective and efficient performance in organizations often arises. Participants in such discussions hasten to point out— and properly so—that history is replete with superstars and that mankind owes countless debts to them.

It happens that many of the world's most outstanding and revered pioneers and innovators achieved great successes either because of, or in spite of, their unconventional, non-conforming, single-minded, or even downright cantankerous natures. Those who wish to downplay the value of relationships in achieving results will glibly ask, "What about Einstein?" or "What about Thomas Edison?" or "What about . . . ?" They might more assertively add comments such as, "I never heard of General Douglas MacArthur or General George Patton ever being credited with being great team players!" (Incidentally, often those are the same people who would say,

"Well, *my* father lived to be 92, and he smoked and drank more heavily than anybody else I know!")

The issue, of course, is *not* an issue of teamwork being a *substitute* for genius, or wisdom, or boundless innovation, or compelling commitment and dedication, or super-human energy, or for unending persistence, or irresistible charisma, or *any other* superlative virtue, including what some might call the propensity for incredible luck! It is a matter of why not both or all?

The need for teamwork may be dependent on timing and circumstances. For example, entrepreneurs often find themselves being incredibly effective in developing start-up companies, but less effective (or even highly ineffective) when the company has grown significantly. During the early stages of a company's growth, a small nucleus of people may be involved in ideation, experimentation or exploration, modification, and demonstration activities in which individual skills and efforts overshadow the needs and opportunities associated with more highly coordinated efforts. Even so, it is likely that early progress will proceed most effectively if the right hand knows what the left hand is doing.

As an organization grows to thirty, forty, fifty and more people, the challenge for teamwork becomes significant. The implementation role in such cases may go beyond the interests or skills of the effective innovator who guided the company initially. There are several alternatives in such cases:

1. The shifting needs of the organization may be left unaddressed, in which case the implementation phase may be followed by deterioration and eventual extinction.
2. The founder or founders may hire someone with operating skill, remaining themselves in development roles where they can continue to enjoy exercising their innovative and creative skills in the same company.
3. If others have gained control of the company, they may set aside or force early retirement of the founder or founders.

4. The founders may step aside on their own initiative—
   often after selling the company or going public—and
   either retire or undertake another start-up.
5. The founder or founders, if sufficiently interested and
   willing to learn, may develop the additional insights,
   skills, and dedication needed to appropriately handle
   operating matters.

The list of great achievers who lend themselves to "Yes,
but . . ." comments is legend.

Columbus discovered America (or did he?) but was unable to prevent discord and conflict among the crews of his
various ships.

Yes, Generals MacArthur and Patton were brilliant strate-
gists and field commanders, but were never held up as examples of great team players.

Henry Ford put much of America on wheels, but he also
presided over union-management disputes resulting not only
in much union-management conflict, but also many deaths.

Charles Lindbergh risked his life to move aviation ahead,
but he had a reputation for being a quiet loner.

It was the genius of Chester Carlson that led to the inven-
tion of xerography, but it was a team of engineers and scien-
tists who brought it to practical status and an additional team
of thousands who helped people acquire and use the equipment.

Igor Sikorsky said, "The work of the individual still remains the spark that moves man forward." The team's function is to assist these individuals, when appropriate, in the
translation of their "sparks" into more broadly effective and
efficient applications and results than would be obtainable
through the resources and efforts of the isolated individuals.

You may have your own favorite list of people who have
become famous or even changed the course of history but
who may not have scored high on teamwork. The point
remains, however, that teamwork is a challenge that has not
been addressed as well as it could (and should) be addressed,

historically or at present. No list of people who succeeded when teamwork was not of the essence, or who became famous when greater teamwork skill might have helped, reduces the challenge that organizations face regarding the effective and efficient integration of people pursuing purposeful endeavors.

You know as well as I do that companies often become bureaucratic and/or autocratic to the extent that superstars and potential superstars find their environments overly restrictive—or even stifling. How many highly talented or high-potential people do you know who have left companies to seek an atmosphere more conducive to their needs? And many, of course, have left to form their own companies. A recent study indicated that the most common goal underlying entrepreneurial efforts was the pursuit of a more stimulating environment and the opportunity to achieve—not the often-assumed pursuit of personal wealth!

Through understanding and mutual respect, peak performance teams learn to accommodate the needs and interests of all types of teammates. They welcome intellectual or technical wizards who may be, but certainly aren't necessarily, introverted or quiet. Considerate associates will not push them toward being more extroverted (or more anything) in ways that might limit their potential innovative contributions.

However, as good team players themselves, these dynamos should continually review their own *total* contribution to the success of the organization. They should welcome feedback and be responsive to it. They should not commit funds that the organization doesn't have or can't afford, or quietly pursue their own interests in so much isolation that they preclude the effective integration of their efforts into the successful pursuit of the company's and group's missions. In essence, those who excel should note the words of Samuel Johnson: "No degree of knowledge attainable by man is able to place him above the need for assistance."

The sensitive team leader will help create an open environment in which associates are empowered to reach out creatively to expand and to improve the scope and quality of the individual contributions of the group's superstars. In essence, he or she will facilitate opportunities for people to achieve and to be recognized. At the same time, the fully effective leader will maintain a communicative, coordinative, and cooperative environment to foster group, as well as individual, success.

Yes, cheers for the superstars. But thanks also to the use of teamwork by those groups who, with or without the help of superstars, have achieved great successes!

Chapter 6

The Blessings and Challenges of Team Member Differences

We didn't all come over in the same ship, but here we are in the same boat.

Unknown

Part of the challenge of pulling a team together is the typical diversity of interests and approaches of its individual members. This diversity also provides opportunity, because it creates a team having different skills and interest levels which are useful in the accomplishment of the team's missions.

The talent and challenging personalities of any team may be infinite, but some of the most often observed types are described below. Any particular individual may fit more than one of these descriptions and play different roles in different circumstances.

Those Who Fill Key Needs of a Group

- **THE PRIME MOVER** may be visionary and is always committed and energetic. Puts the team together, gives it direction, and keeps it moving. Marshals the members with their varied abilities toward effective performance and results.
- **THE UTILITY PLAYER** is somewhat like a utility in-fielder on a baseball team, broadly capable and ready to fill (either officially or unofficially) a variety of the needs of an evolving group. Comforting to have on a team. May or may not be a good Prime Mover.
- **THE POINT OR TRAIL BLAZER** leads the way, cuts the trail, tests the water—and when all's clear, waves to the others to follow.
- **THE PASSIVE FOLLOWER** will take guidance from others, usually quietly and supportively doing what-ever he or she understands the group expects of him or her—but needs to be asked.
- **THE NOTE-TAKER** may or may not play additional roles, but records the vital elements of discussions, decisions, and commitments of the group. May con-tribute substantially to the clear identification of ob-jectives, commitments, progress, and results.
- **THE IMPARTIAL OBSERVER** may generally exam-ine points of view calmly and objectively, or perhaps only when the issue is not of particular interest to him or her. Can help groups achieve balanced evaluations of alternatives.
- **THE MEDIATOR** also serves as conciliator. Can help team members resolve differences constructively, but may be satisfied with smooth interactions even if no progress is made toward results.

People who fill these roles are the ones you can count on to help get things done. These team members drive hard to provide support and other members may tend to favor and defer to them. Such tendencies are natural, but the players should be handled and controlled in ways that keep other team members from feeling sufficiently envious or jealous to create cliques or divisiveness.

Those with Alternate or Distracting Agendas

- **THE CIVIC-MINDED PILLAR's** top priority seems to be seeking out and joining civic endeavors. Likely to bring a wealth of key contacts to the team's table, but may not have time left over to dependably carry out any contributory assignments. May be praised and criticized alternately as "all heart." May talk the talk but not walk the walk.
- **THE PROVERBIAL "YES" PERSON** will cater to authority and would rather agree with virtually anyone than contribute a different opinion or insight at even a small risk.
- **THE HELPFUL RELUCTANT** may be labeled as a martyr. Can be wonderfully willing to help others whenever asked, but usually moans and groans about being picked on too frequently and unfairly. After all the complaining, though, will usually rise to the challenge and respond dependably.
- **THE GUILTY APOLOGIST** may put more effort into apologizing for mistakes than correcting them. May require substantial comforting and support to consider venturing out again into the realm of risk.

Associates with alternate or distracting agendas can be helped with clear goal delineation and periodic reviews of progress toward their goals. They should clearly understand what is expected of them, what priorities exist, what value system governs their freedom to act in pursuing their objectives, and what dates are targeted for intermediate and final progress reviews. If their distracting agendas impede progress, they need to be coached by the team leader. If their idiosyncrasies do not detract from their effectiveness, they need not be addressed. Remember, the ultimate test of teamwork is continued and repeated effectiveness—not conformity or similarity of styles and approaches.

The Under-appreciated

- **THE SACRIFICIAL LAMB** may be the junior or least-skilled member of the group, sent to represent the group at meetings on subjects with which the group leader is unsympathetic. In worst case, is blamed for group's lack of success.
- **THE PARADE SWEEPER** follows in the team's footsteps, cleaning up after his or her associates. Helpful in wrapping up details and handling menial or unpleasant tasks for the group.

By definition, the under-appreciated deserve more kudos. Some managers have told me they don't want to hire anybody who doesn't have the potential to be president or at least a corporate officer. The problem with this thinking is that a pyramidal organizational structure limits upward mobility, even for many of the best people.

If too much emphasis is given to upward mobility and the importance of those at the top of a conventional organization, almost certainly those in junior positions will be viewed inappropriately as "just a secretary," "just a draftsman," "just a janitor," "just a clerk," etc. And you can be sure if they are viewed as "just a whatever," they will sense it. In exciting work environments, *every* individual is recognized as playing a useful role. And when they perform well in their roles, they should be complimented. On the other hand, if the role truly is not useful, that position should be expanded or eliminated.

Those with Territorial Interests

- **THE DEDICATED SUB-OPTIMIZER** has a very narrow focus. Entirely dependable regarding the fulfillment of his or her specific duties, but doesn't see the broad picture. Lacks sensitivity to the potential impact of his or her actions on others.

- **THE NEST GUARDER** is also known as the Protectionist. Extremely conscious of territories or domains and is primarily interested in protecting his or her boundaries from encroachment by others. May also be reluctant to share information freely.
- **THE COMPETITIVE ACTOR** is always concerned about how he or she is perceived by the audience above all else. "How will they view me?" is of more concern to the Actor than the success or failure of the overall effort.

The Dedicated Sub-Optimizer simply may need to gain more insight and understanding of how his or her role fits into the broad picture of the organization and its mission. The Nest Guarder and the Competitive Actor, however, may be insecure and will not likely become strong team players until the sources of their feelings of insecurity are addressed. They could be coached on how to build their levels of self-confidence. They might also need a better understanding of the importance the company places on teamwork—that is, that people who do their best to perform well and cooperatively are going to be supported, coached, and given every reasonable opportunity to succeed.

The Talkers

- **THE ORATOR** usually regales others with his or her poise and facility with words. May carry more influence through style than appropriate for the substance of his or her thoughts, but may do well in presenting the team's position to others.
- **THE MOTOR MOUTH** constantly talks and may or may not contribute ideas that could be piggybacked. Most likely will not take the time to listen to ideas of others, or allow them to be shared.

- **THE TATTLER** will share information with others about what went on in a meeting but likely will disclose elements of discussions, particularly disagreements, that may embarrass others.
- **THE PREACHER** is also known as the Evangelist. Sets high standards for the group, but as the old saying goes, the group may be better off doing as he or she *says* rather than what he or she *does*.

Good facilitators allow for balanced participation and the involvement of others. They also must be goal-oriented and time-conscious. They can help the more vociferous by setting up time allotments for individual agenda items in meetings, by having the most talkative people report at the end of the agenda, and by soliciting the ideas of those who have not been heard from. Tattlers can be coached to look forward to opportunity instead of backward to blame, and all can benefit from constructive feedback regarding how they are being perceived.

The Insulters and Antagonists

- **THE KNOW-IT-ALL** thinks he or she has *all* the answers, so doesn't listen to or remain open for ideas from others. Often very bright. May in fact have great suggestions, but can be insulting and a divisive influence. Rarely, if ever, will accept the loss of an argument.
- **THE PERSISTENT PEST** hones in on one or two issues (perhaps even detailed or minor ones) and won't back off. Can thus cause potentially useful reconsideration, but more likely will be a block or time waster.

Insulters and antagonists are often results- or task-oriented, and they may drive toward completion of immediate task-oriented objectives without any concern for, or attention to, the building of relationships along the way. They need to be coached on the concepts of process as well as content, and on the advantages of principled behavior that provide for the modest up-front time and effort investment that may be needed to enhance the approach being used. It also may help to team them with others who are highly skilled on process matters so that others can help them in their interactions.

The Unique but Useful

- **THE PERFECTIONIST** is never satisfied, even with excellence. Likely to suffer from analysis paralysis, but may take the group one step higher in the quality of its final efforts.
- **THE IMPRACTICAL DREAMER** is likely to offer highly innovative and often unconventional suggestions. May contribute to extending the horizons of the group's focus, but may also need support or reinforcement when ideas are criticized by others.
- **THE QUIET WIZARD** is broadly knowledgeable and/or experienced. Great as a fountain of knowledge which can be tapped by the group. Unlike the Know-It-All, likely to be passive, needing to be brought out by others desiring to tap into his or her wisdom.

These unique but useful types can help stretch a group to higher levels of achievement. The challenge is to encourage their input and to do so with a sufficiently open and responsive group to assure a reasonable portion of their suggestions are utilized or implemented. An alternate approach is to set them up in special groups with innovative efforts as their prime function while others focus on ensuring effective and efficient implementation of daily tasks. To maintain a high level of spirit for those not on the special innovation teams, the work of the special teams should be seen as an addition to, not instead of, any innovative efforts within operating groups.

The Makers—and Avoiders—of Decisions

- **THE RISK TAKER** is likely to be highly optimistic. Will tend to innovate—even, perhaps, beyond prudent limits. A plus factor to expanding the potential contribution of a group beyond expectations, but best utilized with some scrutiny or control.
- **THE DICTATOR** wants to make decisions and tell others to carry them out. Likely to view other team members as valuable only for implementation, not idea generation. Focus may be exclusively on tasks with no regard for relationships. May even be arrogant and domineering.
- **THE PROCRASTINATOR** never seems to get around to doing what he or she knows should be done or has committed to do. May be helpful in delineating commitments for group members, but needs follow-up by someone else who understands that after all is said and done, more may be said than done.

Whereas the Procrastinator needs to be prodded, the Risk Taker may need to be slowed down and to have prudent limits defined. Regardless of their propensity to move quickly or cautiously, though, decision-makers of all types should be helped to understand that dictatorial announcements of decisions don't tend to win friends and build the ranks of followers among their associates. Good decision-makers involve others who are in positions to help with the quality of the decisions, who will be carrying out the decisions, and who will be impacted by the decisions. They learn to gather an appropriate amount of information and include appropriate levels of involvement, and then they move expeditiously toward implementation.

The Spirit Dampeners

- **THE DARK CLOUD** is sometimes referred to as the Gloom and Doom Purveyor or the Hand Wringer. Always worried and constantly views a glass as half empty—never half full. Can be cynical. However, can help a group see and understand potential down-side consequences of its plans or actions.

- **THE IMPATIENT FIDGETER** is restless, fidgety, constantly glancing at his or her watch, and otherwise exhibiting irritation with any person or thing that might appear to slow the group's progress. Can help contribute a sense of urgency to group, but may also be annoying to others.
- **THE ICEBERG** lacks warmth. Impersonal, not the least interested in nonbusiness conversation of any kind. Often uncomfortable for others to be around, but likely to help the group stay focused on its mission.
- **THE BIG "I"** sees (or appears to see) self as the center of the universe. May have strong drive for results and recognition, but likely to offend others by excessive use of "I" when "we" would be more appropriate.
- **THE HERO** is overly conscious of and thrives on recognition. May want to bask in glory—even undeserved glory. May maintain focus on progress or success, but often will claim more than a fair share of credit.

Managers often are reluctant to address the spirit dampeners, rationalizing instead that they may make valuable contributions on task-related issues. The progressive leader, though, will consider not just the potential positive impact of the spirit dampeners, but also the negative impact on others, and on balance, the possible net loss of effectiveness for the organization as a whole.

The spirit dampeners may respond to guidance from counselors in the human resources department (or professionals outside the company). They may also respond well to systems which provide for anonymous and confidential surveys of one's associates, compilation of the data, and then private consultative feedback to the subject of the survey.

The Dominant Forces and Immovable Objects

- **THE MOVING FREIGHT TRAIN** has momentum in a particular direction. Can be wonderfully helpful if his or her direction is compatible with the needs of the group—but, like a train, may roll over others.
- **THE ROCK OF GIBRALTAR** likes things as they are. "Ain't goin' nowhere, and ain't goin' to change nohow!" Is in the way. Highly and clearly visible and frustratingly unmoving. Others may have to navigate around him or her.
- **THE DEFENSIVE TACKLER** aggressively tries to *get* in the way. Wants to block group progress unless it shifts to a direction more compatible with his or her own scoring interest.
- **THE TRADER** may give a little, but always expects something in return for trading his or her support. The extent of his or her flexibility is always related to the perception of "what's in it for me."

Those who can be categorized as dominant forces or immovable objects potentially are more harmful to an organization's health than the spirit dampeners. They tend to be more visible and they more overtly exhibit behaviors that are counterproductive to the successful performance of the group. The ways to help them are similar to those used to guide the spirit dampeners, but there may be a more urgent need to initiate improvement efforts.

The Major Challenges

- **THE ALLIGATOR** chews people up. Viewed by others as a nasty, impersonal carnivore who seems to delight in vicious attacks on others. Clearly a negative influence.
- **THE BIGOT** will tend to succumb to prejudices and then attempt to explain and/or justify prejudicial behavior intellectually. Very likely to cause or to

enhance substantially the formation of irrationally distinct subgroups within the overall organization.

- **THE JUGGLER** tries to keep too many balls in the air. Likely to arrive late to one meeting and have to leave early, only to arrive late at the next meeting.
- **THE TENDER FLOWER** is delicate. Easily hurt if an issue is taken personally. This person may inhibit open, frank exchanges, but may also cause group members to attempt to remain more civil than they might otherwise. May be crushed by Alligators or other strong types.

The major challenges are, in fact, *major* challenges. The Alligator and Bigot can seriously damage the long-term effectiveness of organizations. The Juggler can negatively impact the performance of others and may also be on the way to a stroke or heart attack. The Tender Flower may be in more personal jeopardy than a factor in jeopardizing the health of the organization—except that he or she may require extraordinary attention, support, and reinforcement in order to survive. Corrective approaches can be similar to those used with the spirit dampeners and the dominant forces or immovable objects.

The Useless Baggage

- **THE SPIRITED WATER SPIDER** is eager, willing, but indiscriminately active. Flits speedily in one direction then another, changing at the slightest influence of others. Can't stay focused. Likely to be spread thin and may lead associates off on tangents.
- **THE SCATTERBRAIN** is just not with it. Can't get focused. Highly malleable and unpredictable.
- **THE JOVIAL CLOWN** is always upbeat, usually smiling, typically lighthearted, and seldom dedicated to helping to achieve the group's mission. Can contribute to the defusing of conflict-laden atmosphere. However, may cause group to substitute fun for focus.

- **THE PRIMPER** uses meeting times to check hairdo, makeup, or clothing. More concerned with personal appearance than group performance. May also distract group members by flirting.
- **THE FLIRT** sees the group as a vehicle to (or facilitator of) romance, so loves to attend meetings. In the extreme, can be a hazard to other group members, the cohesiveness of the group, and even the general welfare of the organization as a whole.
- **THE CAT-NAPPER** may need medical help or perhaps just more sleep at night. If symptoms are sporadic, may simply be bored. Not likely to be a positive factor unless he or she can be kept involved in the conversation.

The useless baggage types often survive through personal charm. They frequently are likeable, but often can be likened to attractive and well-groomed horses that can keep pace with the team, but don't pull any of the load. As with those in prior groups, better feedback and guidance may help. However, because those who are useless baggage may be pleasant and inoffensive, they may not be seen as challenges worthy of high-priority attention. A good, sound, fair approach to goals and controls typically will help illuminate inadequacies and improve the probability that their performance (or lack thereof) will be addressed appropriately.

The Teammate of Our Dreams

The Perfect Teammate: Have You Ever Known One?

Managers might as well accept and enjoy an attitude of "Vive la difference." However, if they wish to establish and maintain high levels of teamwork, they should heed the succinct motto of the Three Musketeers: "All for one, and one for all!" With all the differences that need to be coordinated and reconciled, teamwork obviously requires high priority and much attention if it is going to work.

Often these different types of members in groups have not been effectively integrated into smoothly functioning organizations. One of the major reasons has been that many groups focus so heavily on the pursuit of tasks (or things) that little, or at least much less, attention has been given to people (or relationships). Many of these organizations don't have any mission statement. Others have mission statements outlining the organization's desire to lead in technology or in customer satisfaction, but omitting any mention of commitment to employee motivation and teamwork. Others do include matters relating to the work environment in their mission statements, but then neglect them in practice.

In peak-performance organizations, decision-makers pay substantial attention not just to goals and controls, but also to process versus content and to principle versus expedience (as discussed in the next chapter). They also provide for open communication and extensive feedback on progress as well as needs for improvement (as covered in Chapters 22 and 23). The chapters that follow, and in particular those just mentioned, provide additional guidance on how to capitalize on the challenges associated with team member differences.

Chapter 7

Our Basic Challenge: Individual Expedience

How is it we can find time to do it over, but not the time to do it right initially?

Proverb

When teamwork breaks down, there may be any number of contributing factors. In every instance of inadequate teamwork, however, there are likely to be elements of two underlying causes. The first is *individualism*. One or more individuals will have focused too much on their own narrow needs and interests and not enough on those of the organization as a whole. The second is *expedience*. Any individuals not contributing effectively to the team's endeavors will almost certainly be pursuing expedient courses of action instead of more principled approaches that might better serve longer-term, comprehensive objectives and strategies.

Any or all of the behavioral patterns described in the prior chapter may exist among the constituents of a group. These individual differences compound the challenge of teamwork, but they also create the opportunity to marshal a variety of skills to help assure the accomplishment of the group's mission. What a dull world this would be if everyone thought and acted the same!

Our challenge as leaders in pursuit of improved effectiveness and efficiency through teamwork is *not* to have all our associates think and act the same or similarly, but to have them, in spite of their differences, become more committed to the group's long-term purpose! Whatever his or her nature, each player will contribute more effectively to the extent that he or she can be helped to become

- clearly aware of the group's mission,
- sensitive to individual differences,
- willing to listen to others' views,
- considerate of others' interests and needs,
- interested in the challenges and opportunities of associates, *and*
- oriented to long-term progress and success.

In Chapter 5, credit is given to the past and potential contributions of superstars. It is a fortunate group that can boast of having one or more superstars, but it can only be a winning group if *all* of its members, *including* the superstars, work together in pursuing the group's mission.

The watch/gear analogy demonstrated how good people are a necessary (but not sufficient) element for outstanding group performance. Like the finely-shaped watch gears, good people must work together if the organization is to be effective. Imagine the bedlam at a symphony if each musician played whatever, however, and whenever he or she wished! It is not just the skill of each talented musician that allows a fine orchestra to stir its audience—it is also their skill in playing harmoniously.

Small groups represent an additional coordinating challenge, because it is easier for almost all individuals to identify more closely with associates in smaller groups than with others in a larger group. A violinist is likely to develop stronger ties to others in the string section than to the orchestra as a whole, but the strings as a group must think and act beyond their section for the orchestra to flourish.

So we see that the leader who places teamwork high in his or her priorities should be alert to the propensity of individuals to pursue their own interests and the interests of their closely knit subgroups. These natural tendencies need to be recognized as givens. The successful team leader will see that existing individual and subgroup objectives will be compatible with the needs for coordinated overall effectiveness.

I was once asked to commend a manager's efforts to develop competition between his departments. I couldn't (or wouldn't), and he was somewhat disappointed. I explained that competition was already there. If the departments are capable, good people will take pride in their own accomplishments without any encouragement to do so. On the contrary, the tendency for individuals to focus first clearly on themselves, and next on the interests of their smaller group or unit, can become counterproductive. The teamwork challenge is to harness the enthusiasm of each individual and subgroup in such ways that they complement each other in the effective pursuit of the *organization's* overall mission. And to be fully effective, the enthusiasm, decisions, and efforts of the group should be *principled,* filling the longer-term needs of the organization, and not just providing expedient short-term gratification.

What about the issue of expedience? Probably the most common smoke screens thrown up by someone guilty of an oversight in teamwork are "I didn't have time" or "I was so busy with the crisis that I couldn't take time to bring you into the loop."

When otherwise good people use these excuses, it is awfully easy for most managers to accept their comments and to focus on the next project to be pursued, leaving the appropriate review of the inadequate teamwork process unexplored.

Clearly a violinist could play more notes if he or she didn't pause periodically to let other instruments make their contributions. A plant manager might reduce his direct labor costs by producing long runs without interruption if he or she didn't defer to a request by the sales department in behalf of a customer with an emergency. An engineer might design a product more quickly if he or she didn't take time to discuss how it will be produced. And space shuttles could be launched sooner if those involved didn't worry about safety.

In Chapter 4, it was noted that teamwork, like a fine lawn, requires great effort to establish. To achieve effective teamwork, group members (and group leaders in particular) must raise matters of teamwork in their consciousness and allocate high priority to their pursuit. Time and effort need to be invested in teamwork—both to achieve it and to maintain it.

At a management retreat involving about twenty executives from one of the largest companies in the United States, the participants discussed the company's mission statement. Included among the elements of the statement was an item about fostering career opportunities for the organization's people. During their discussion, one of the executives commented he had a confession to make: "In spite of our mission statement, I have delayed or tried to block transfers or promotions for some of my best people because I haven't wanted to face the inconvenience of having to replace them with less capable or less experienced people. I wonder . . . am I alone in this regard?" Before long, virtually everyone admitted to making similarly expedient self-serving staffing decisions! On the positive side, they unanimously committed themselves to more principled teamwork decisions in the future.

When teamwork is not given high priority and specific periodic attention in an organization, each team member is likely to pursue his or her own narrow commitments. Each will not necessarily intentionally neglect the appropriate involvement of others, but nevertheless will often leave a trail of decisions that can cause extra problems to other team members, limiting the overall potential success of the endeavor.

Taking an expedient approach may be easier in the short run, and may even provide a perverse pleasure for some people! If, for instance, an associate has made a mistake or done something you didn't like, you might enjoy a surge of satisfaction by telling your associate off. This expedient, knee-jerk reaction, though, might leave you with subsequent regrets about your own behavior—and almost certainly would jeopardize your relationship with that associate.

You may drive hard for Results with a capital "R." The way you handle others along the way will determine your success with another important consideration for the cultivation of long-term effectiveness—and that is Relationships, also with a capital "R!" In some circles, R&R means "Rest and Recreation." In building teamwork, R&R means "Relationships as well as Results."

Although it is almost always quicker and often easier in the short run to go for results *now,* in the long run an organization's results will usually be maximized if relationships are strong and positive. By maintaining good relationships, team members can help each other time after time in their quests for superior performance and will find satisfaction in that:

T *ogether*
E *ach*
A *chieves*
M *ore*
S *uccess!*

The point here is that individuals (whether or not superstars) have an opportunity to drive for results in one of two ways. They can pursue tasks without regard for process (or relationships)—making demands of others, neglecting to keep other interested parties informed, criticizing others, or even competitively undermining other individuals or departments in a dedicated dash for glory. (Unfortunately, our studies have shown that the short-run path, at least to the level of neglect or oversight, is taken more often than not.)

Or the path to achievement on a particular task could be a path across a fine teamwork lawn. On this path, those in pursuit of objectives will maintain relationships by being considerate, understanding, and supportive of others, taking pride in their own contributions to success. They do so not only in the pursuit of any particular task, but also in the simultaneous preservation or enhancement of a level of team spirit that will boost the chances of future successes as well. They frequently and constantly rededicate themselves to becoming successful teams.

When teamwork prevails, the violinists are happy to supplement and complement the efforts of the woodwind and percussion sections, and vice versa. The plant manager sees requests to interrupt the smooth flow of production in behalf of a customer emergency as an opportunity instead of a nuisance. The engineers welcome the involvement of others during the early design stages, recognizing that well-designed products must be both producible and functionally sound.

Individuals have to think beyond their own narrow interests to the interests of other individuals and the long-term principled interests of the organization as a whole—that's what teamwork is all about! For a team player, or one who aspires to improved team playing, "A Teamwork Pledge" is appropriate.

Instead of moving ahead expediently on their own, true team members habitually ask themselves these three key questions:

1. Who could provide information that could help me (us) make a better decision?
2. Who will have to carry out the decision?
3. Who will be impacted by the decision?

An additional question is pertinent to the teamworker's decision-making process: Would it be beneficial to the achievement of our organization's mission if these other peo-

---

A TEAMWORK PLEDGE

While diligently pursuing the fulfillment of my own responsibilities as an individual contributor or supervisor of
others, I will, with equal diligence, pursue opportunities to be
communicative and cooperative. I will also be supportive and
understanding of others as we collectively pursue the effective and efficient achievement of our organization's goals.

---

ple were more involved in my (our) decision making process?
Usually, the answer will be a resounding "Yes!"

Good team-oriented decision-makers soon learn that it is
important to raise these questions *early* in the decision making process. Preferably, these questions should be asked at
the very beginning. The danger in waiting arises from our
tendency to get a preliminary solution in mind and then,
because of the presence of the preliminary solution, be less
receptive to information that might point toward some
other—and perhaps better—alternative.

Goals and controls. Process versus content. Principle versus expedience. Good team players keep these basic concepts in mind. And they place *very high priority* on using *good
processes* as they pursue *highly principled decision-making*.
They recognize that by doing the right things properly the first
time, they are less likely to have to make the time to do them
over later.

Chapter 8

The Golden Rule and Poor Mr. Guillotin

Do unto others as you would have them do unto you.

The Golden Rule

Who is Joseph Guillotin—and what does he have to do with the Golden Rule?

He was a French physician, born in 1738. As a member of the French National Assembly during the French Revolution, he was a staunch supporter of a law that proposed the use of a machine to carry out executions. It was his name that was placed on the instrument that provided a more efficient means of decapitation—an instrument that became one of the best-known symbols of the French Revolution.

Normally authors give the birth and death dates of historical figures at the same time. But I delayed the disclosure of the second date to place additional emphasis on the date of his death in 1814. It is popularly believed that he was executed—in public—by the use of—you guessed it—the very machine whose use he so strongly advocated. We might conclude that his story is a captivating (or decapitating) illustration of the adage: "What goes around comes around."

The concept of compromise ("I'll meet you half way!") is as American as motherhood and apple pie. The problem is, the meet-you-half-way concept isn't nearly as strong a concept or commitment as is the Golden Rule. It creates vulnerable relationships that are jeopardized each time one of the parties believes that the other hasn't quite contributed a fair share.

A more admirable approach, and one that will foster strong team relationships, is for each party to seek every opportunity to help the others. It isn't easy to develop habits along these lines, but this approach nevertheless must be pursued to foster teamwork.

According to the Golden Rule, we should do unto others as we would have them do unto us. This doesn't say that we should follow the Golden Rule as long as others follow it or that we should follow it a little bit if we think others are only following it a little bit. It simply says we should treat others as we would like to be treated—period! Without qualification! And without holding back until they demonstrate a team spirit to match our own.

You probably have heard that what goes around comes around. This cliché holds true with regard to relationships and to teamwork. If I am considerate and supportive of you, you will tend to interact similarly with me—maybe not right away if you haven't been used to good teamwork and maybe not to an extent that matches my positive team efforts. If the general working atmosphere is at all positive, though, you almost certainly will pick up at least *some* of my considerate and supportive behavior. The big danger is that I will give up too soon if you are slow or limited in your constructive response and if my sense of fairness has been stretched to its limit.

Unfortunately, once I give up on you, I will tend to withdraw into my own world, do my own thing, and regrettably take the "teamwork-be-damned" attitude. If I take this attitude consciously, I will be able to justify and rationalize my behavior on the basis that I did try, but you just didn't do your share. Then you and I will likely both lose.

Tough and inequitable as it may seem, if we are to foster high levels of teamwork, each of us must be dedicated to making it happen—and not just if the others we are dealing with do likewise, or "meet us half way." The pursuit of teamwork must not be seen as a matter of fairness, but as a matter worthy of pursuit *forever*, in and of itself. In short, it should be an *absolute*, not a relative, commitment for each of us.

One of our real challenges in life is to be able to see ourselves as others see us, or to view ourselves with more objectivity than most people can bring to bear. At performance review time, the supervisor's challenge in communicating with his or her associate is compounded by the widespread tendency people have to view themselves through rose-colored glasses. In fact, studies have shown that for any positive trait, 85% of us will think that we are above average!

Similarly, in our work on teamwork we have *never* found *anyone* who didn't wish that *other* people or departments would be more communicative and cooperative with them. It was on the basis of these observations that I developed the previously mentioned law of communication within organizations:

In whichever department you work, you and your department associates wish the people in the other departments would communicate, coordinate, and co-operate with you more!

The issue each of us needs to consider is: Who are all these people who don't communicate and cooperate with each other? Isn't it just possible that *they* are *us?* In fact, who else could they be? And, if we are going to improve, why don't we each accept full responsibility for at least maximizing our own level of communication and cooperation? With positive orientation to each other, we can generate true "win-

win "interactions. We can, in fact, benefit from the concept of "what goes around comes around."

Even the selfish might heed Ralph Waldo Emerson's inspiring message:

It is one of the most beautiful compensations of this life that no person can sincerely try to help another without helping himself.

Poor Mr. Guillotin! Perhaps his is one of history's most graphic examples of "What goes around comes around."

Winning Plays And Strategies

So, we have seen that good people can be poor team players, whether their teams are athletic teams or other types of organizations or groups.

In this section we will look at covering the basics. When your favorite football team loses a game, they probably have not done well on the basics, such as missing their blocks and tackles. Or, in industry and commerce, employees may have worked very diligently, but in pursuit of the wrong goal.

Effective nonathletic teams cover their basics well. They rise above constant crisis-management activities to emphasize teamwork and long-term results. The members clarify objectives, select and promote people carefully, train and delegate, and use tightly run meetings effectively. Covering such basics is the thrust of this next section.

Chapter 9

Observations about Truths in Team Sports

Build with your team a feeling of oneness, of dependence on one another, and of strength derived from unity in the pursuit of your objective.

Vince Lombardi

Sports enthusiasts know that their teams must pursue certain fundamental truths if they are to win more consistently than their competitors. Effective coaches follow these guidelines and constantly push their players to behave accordingly. These basics are:

1. Know your objectives.
2. Know the rules.
3. Know what is expected of you in your position.
4. Understand the relationship of your position to other positions.
5. Practice, practice, and practice how to do things right.
6. Maintain dedicated self-discipline.
7. Get and develop the best talent you can.

8. Welcome new teammates enthusiastically and supportively.
9. Coach or guide constructively when a mistake is made.
10. Assess both individual and team strengths and weaknesses periodically.
11. Help less effective team members improve, or if appropriate, help them withdraw or retire gracefully.
12. Make principled decisions that will benefit the team not just minute by minute, but game after game, and season after season.

When we think about these fundamentals and their implications regarding the quality of team endeavors, we are inclined to visualize their application to such sports as football, soccer, baseball, basketball, hockey, and volleyball, all of which require highly coordinated interplay among team members. However, even swim and track teams can apply these basics. Team strategy often requires that some swimmers or runners participate in "off" events to maximize the team's score. And, obviously, coordinated team effort is required for optimal performance in relays.

These guidelines also are appropriate for developing effectiveness in groups of _all_ kinds, whether they be professional, industrial, commercial, governmental, religious, philanthropic, or volunteer. Most sports enthusiasts with whom I have shared this list support it, yet incredibly, they don't pay enough attention to many, most, or all of these points in the pursuit of their nonathletic endeavors!

Know Your Objectives

Participants should know and clearly understand their team's objectives. In a pre-season game, how critical is it to win? Do we want a large number of players to participate so we'll have a chance to see them in action? Will our game strategy be conservative and calculated or to "go for broke" at every opportunity? In our businesses, are we interested in increasing our share of the market, gross margins, profit as a percent of sales, profit relative to investment, total amount of profit, or cash flow during the next year? Two years? Five years? If we don't individually and collectively know the objectives and their priorities, how can we maximize our effectiveness in playing the game?

Know the Rules

We should all know what our degrees of freedom are as we drive toward our objectives. How will the score be kept, and how do we avoid penalties that might slow our progress or invalidate a scoring effort? What are the organization's policies, procedures, and practices? To what laws or regulations must we conform? And, under what circumstances, if any, am I free to use my own judgment in circumventing our policies or procedures?

Know What Is Expected

In addition to understanding where the organization is headed, each member should understand his or her role clearly. What is the basic description of my position? What specifically do you expect of me? What will constitute outstanding, good, acceptable, poor, and unacceptable levels of performance in my role? To avoid my thinking, talking, or acting on the basis of "that's not my job," am I expected to "perform other duties as requested," and should I also "attend to additional matters as deemed appropriate"?

Understand Your Position

Under normal circumstances, how should I fulfill my basic responsibilities so I facilitate—or at least don't impede—the efforts of my associates in fulfilling theirs? Are there other situations that may arise during which I should adjust my approach? If we have a new, inexperienced player or associate in one of our positions, should I take this into consideration in how I approach my own role? In the event that one of my teammates drops the ball, or if one of my associates does something ineffectively or inappropriately, how should I react? May I, or should I, temporarily step out of my conventional role to help elsewhere? Sensitivity to these and similar questions will help the team develop cohesiveness and more consistent effectiveness. Each person will assist others and be able to count on assistance from others so that together we will more successfully forge ahead regardless of circumstances.

Practice, Practice, Practice

It would be unthinkable for a school or professional team to play without pre-season practices and between-game workouts. Similarly, as organizations go from opportunity to opportunity, from problem to problem, and from crisis to crisis, they can benefit from preventive, anticipatory, and remedial training. What kinds of challenges are we likely to face? Can any of them be prevented from arising? If they arise anyway, will we know how to respond? Are there ways for us to practice in simulated circumstances during which the stakes aren't so high as in real life? The most beneficial team development now being pursued in business is highly participative, giving the team members an opportunity to practice and to develop skills so they can meet the organization's challenges.

Maintain Self-Discipline

The self-disciplined person or group will do what is necessary or important, not just those things that are most convenient or pleasant. Attention to process (relationship) issues and training can be postponed. Have we dedicated ourselves to the improvement of our approach, or are we so busy playing a game that we won't take time for a lesson? Are we so busy shooting that we don't take time to learn how to aim?

Are we spending much of our time and effort trying to redo things that we didn't learn how to do properly at the outset? It takes discipline to think before we act, to do the important as well as the pleasant, and to do the difficult as well as the easy. It also takes discipline to make tough decisions along a principled route instead of being diverted onto expedient short-cuts. Improvement and progress often are not easy to come by. As most athletes learn very early in their training: "No pain, no gain."

Get and Develop Talent

Teams are dynamic entities. They grow and they shrink. Members are promoted, or they quit, retire, die, or are removed. Some, like the old soldier, just fade away. Organizations that prosper most in the long run will constantly watch for—and assertively seek—the best talent they can find to fill their growth and replacement vacancies. What capabilities do we need? What types of individuals are most likely to meet our expectations? Where can we find them? How can we get their attention and entice them to join us? How can we make better selection decisions, and hence fewer costly hiring mistakes? This process of analyzing needs, recruiting candidates, and sorting the eagles from the turkeys is one in which most sports-oriented organizations outperform their business counterparts year after year!

Welcome New Teammates

One of the most fragile aspects of teamwork relates to the potential perception of new talent as a threat to the careers, security, and welfare of the longer-term members of the team. The team or group wishing to succeed in its mission should welcome new talent and help newcomers get integrated as effective contributors to the team's endeavors. Who is this newcomer, and what does he or she need to know to feel a part of us? How can I help this person feel comfortable or get oriented? How could I make it easier for this person to get off to a good start with the others in our group? Generally, small amounts of attention given to these questions by the established members of a group will have substantial positive impact on the newcomer and will contribute significantly to building or improving mutually beneficial relationships for the years ahead.

Coach Constructively

Since none of us is perfect and since what goes around comes around, we will all enhance our individual and collective contributions to success if we jump at opportunities to help when one of us is floundering. The true team player will help others avoid embarrassment, learn from mistakes, and build testimonials of progress out of tests of abilities. What isn't working quite right, and why? Can I help and is there some way I could show how we could do better next time? Was there anything that I did (or didn't do) that in any way could have contributed to this difficulty? As these "lessons learned" and related questions are pursued, it is beneficial to look forward to opportunity rather than backward to blame. Enhancing the strength of our group and the outlook for our future should remain foremost among all our priorities.

Assess Strengths and Weaknesses

Athletic teams will often review game films to learn more accurately what was done well or not so well. Are there discernible patterns regarding what seems to work best for us? How about patterns of things we have not handled well? What seems to be causing our successes? Our failures or delays? Should we more frequently step back and objectively review how we are going about the business of our business? Many firms set aside half days or several days periodically to shift the focus from meeting today's deadlines today and tomorrow's deadlines tomorrow (results) to review how deadlines are set and pursued and how they might be undertaken more effectively (for example, issues of process or relationships). Someone has suggested these sessions, often referred to as management retreats, might more appropriately be called management advances.

Help Less Effective Team Members

There is no reason mutually constructive communication, coordination, and cooperation should exist just for those on the way in and up, to the exclusion of those on their way down or out. Each individual will feel better, and the team will be much more likely to exhibit high morale, if principled approaches are used in place of expediency as people leave the mainstream of the organization. How can each of us and the group better anticipate career moves? Beyond developing better foresight, what could or should each of us do to facilitate transitions, improving them from the point of view of both the individual and the organization? Through mutual consideration and such techniques as succession planning, these transitions can be accomplished more effectively. Those who are floundering can be guided or coached more than is usually done, and retirees can be allowed to retain part-time employment or roles as consultants as they and the organization adjust to their more complete withdrawal.

Make Principled Decisions

Principled decisions usually are not as easy to make as expedient ones. In fact, it is precisely their ease which makes expedient decisions more common than correct. It is easier to *not* address the player who hits a home run when disobeying an instruction to bunt. And it may be easier to support someone who has done well in his or her own department, even though the approach used seriously impacted one or more other departments. But each day we should ask ourselves if what we are doing is proper for the long run as well as for the moment. Have I been honest with everyone I've dealt with today? Do I really intend to follow through? Have I viewed the needs of all the members of the group? Do I really feel that I am solving a problem, or am I just postponing it? Do I believe in what I am doing, or do I have to try to justify it—even to myself? In short, when I go to bed at night, do I feel good about what I did today and what I will be doing tomorrow?

On Teamwork

The purpose of an organization is to achieve overall effectiveness, not just the effective performance of individuals or subgroups. We must all strive to do well individually, yet always with a focus on the overall needs of the organization.

Everybody, according to Tolstoy, wants to change humanity—but nobody wants to change himself or herself. We must look for ways to compliment and support others, not blame one another for our difficulties.

Anybody can be dedicated to long hours, hard work, and individual effectiveness, and can feel good about that contribution. The true issue, however, is the extent to which we contribute to the goals and results of the organization as a whole.

Management must recognize people's tendencies to identify with groups as well as the extent to which they quickly develop small group loyalties. One of management's key challenges, therefore, is to help broaden the scope of vision beyond the interests of the individual unit, department, or division.

We will never be better as a company than we are to each other. As we look beyond our conveniently narrow horizons, we should continually ask how we can be of help, and we should never implement a change without previously reviewing it with others who might be affected by the change.

Opportunities to help one another, person-to-person and department-to-department, are all around us. They are amazingly easy to find if we watch for them and if we make it a habit to ask people in other departments how they are doing and how we can be of help.

Real teamwork can be so gratifying that it may be considered reward enough. Nevertheless, the individual who habitually communicates, coordinates, and cooperates with others will be recognized by associates as an invaluable asset.

Knowledge of where the organization is headed, what each individual's general role is in the overall endeavor, and what specific objectives particular groups are expected to achieve is extremely important. For optimal success of the organization, however, a spirit of teamwork is absolutely essential!

Chapter 10

How Teamwork Works

*We would rather have one man or
woman working with us than three
merely working for us.*

F.W. Woolworth

As a high school athlete I sat in an auditorium at the year's first all-student convocation. As clearly as if it were a few minutes ago, I can remember the way our principal stood before us with his shirtsleeves turned up. He held a long pencil in both hands and effortlessly broke it in half. He then broke another and another and another.

To complete his memorable demonstration, he counted out twenty-two more pencils to represent our football team and bound them together with a rubber band at each end. Then he held the bundled pencils out toward the students. With substantial apparent effort he tried to break the bundle as he had done the individual pencils, but without success.

For dramatic effect to reinforce his point, he handed the bundle of pencils to the biggest, strongest, toughest tackle on the football team and challenged him to break them. He couldn't. The point had been made.

As George P. Morris said during the formative years of the United States, "United we stand, divided we fall."

In addition to being useful in mutually protective or defensive situations, teamwork can facilitate collective achievements that defy individual accomplishments. Military forces and gym classes alike practice building human pyramids to boost individuals over walls too high to be reached by any individual. After the first team members get to the top, they in turn pull their remaining team members up, and the team meets its scaling challenge.

These cases illustrate extreme situations of all-versus-nothing opportunities for teamwork. But every day in every group (company, volunteer organization, religious group, etc.), there are less dramatic opportunities for team members to expend a little more effort to assist others. The wonderfully synergistic result often is the translation of this slight extra consideration and concern for others into substantial increases in overall effectiveness.

Basic thoughts? You bet. Simple concepts? Certainly. It's not that the development or improvement of teamwork involves particularly complex concepts, it's just that it doesn't happen automatically. Now that we've observed truths about teamwork in sports, for an understanding of their business applicability it is time to undergo the equivalent of "basic training" to get teamwork going.

Let's look into a typical day in the life of Tom Teamworthy, the operations manager for the Cooperative Manufacturing Company. As Tom approaches the guard gate, he is greeted by the guard's smile and a motion to drive on in —but Tom rolls down his window and comes to a stop.

"Morning, George. How was your game last night?"

"Hey, terrific! We won!"

"Good. See you later," Tom replies as he drives on.

In addition to being a good team player, Tom also delegates and manages his time well. However, in preparation for an out-of-town trip tomorrow, he had taken home two bulky budget files along with his briefcase. As Tom puts his briefcase down and fumbles with the files while locking his car, he hears the pleasant voice of Sam, the company's sales manager.

"Hi, Tom. Let me give you a hand."

"Sam, what a break! Thanks!"

"Looks like you took a chunk of the office with you last night."

"Sure did. I'm wrestling with some budget issues for next year's plan, and I haven't been able to sort things out as completely as I'd like yet."

Sam takes the files from Tom, and as they walk into the building Sam comments, "By the way, Tammy was a great help to us yesterday afternoon. She tracked down some information we needed for a special order for Colossal Customer Corporation."

Tammy is seated at her desk when the men arrive.

"Good morning, Tammy."

"Hi, Tom. Hi, Sam."

"Hi, Tammy. I was just telling Tom about how you jumped in to help us yesterday. Thanks again."

"You're welcome, Sam. Anytime."

As Sam puts down the files and starts to leave, Tom thanks him for being his temporary porter and for his supportive comments about Tammy. He then begins to review the day's schedule with Tammy. He tells Tammy he would like to take a quick walk through the factory before the monthly staff meeting at 9:00 a.m.

"If anybody needs me, just page."

The phone rings just as Tom starts to walk away, and Tammy calls after him that it's Pete, the president, calling long distance. Pete says he just wanted to commend Tom on his good performance last month.

"Thanks, Pete. It's always good to be appreciated, but it wasn't me; it was our gang. They're good people, and they're really giving it their full efforts. We just need to get them a little better coordinated and a little more supportive of each other, and they'll be formidable!"

They conclude their brief conversation, and Tom gets back to his walk through the plant. Today, however, because of the phone delay and the pending staff meeting, his tour is a little faster than normal. As is his practice, though, he does keep at least a brief tour high in his priorities. He uses MBWA (management by walking around) as a way of staying visible and in touch with all levels of the organization. As he walks around in his shirtsleeves, he demonstrates his accessibility and personal interfacing skills.

The staff meeting for the operations group takes its normal course, with each department head making his or her report before Tom gives his overview comments. It's Frank's turn to report in his role as the manager of planning and financial analysis.

"I have two things to cover today. First is just a reminder that we've been on time for each milestone so far in our planning cycle for next year, and our next target date is next Wednesday for your initial capital expenditure plans or requests."

"Thanks for the reminder, Frank. Does anyone have any questions on Frank's first item? . . . No questions? O.K., what about your other point, Frank?"

"Well, the second thing I want to cover is a problem Mike and I have been discussing . . . uh . . . debating, about the need for him to get his monthly reports to me promptly."

"Excuse me, Frank," Tom interjects, "but is this something you and Mike can work out on your own or with my help? Maybe we don't have to tie up the rest of the group on it or is the issue more general, involving a number of us?"

"Well, uh, yeah . . . we, uh, I guess we can handle it separately."

"O.K., let's move on to Sam's report on sales and marketing."

Sam gives a mostly up-beat report on sales and the outlook for the next six months, but he points out that dealers continue to complain about the inconvenience and confusion of back orders because of the continuing problem of out-of-stock parts.

During the discussion that follows, Mike points out that the inventory value in general has been about as planned, but that because of delivery problems from a key vendor there are an abnormally high number of parts and subassemblies that are out-of-stock. Various alternatives are discussed, and Mike commits to reducing the number of out-of-stock parts to 1% in thirty days. Tom wraps up the discussion.

"Good, Mike. That sounds like an ambitious commitment, but it's important, as we all know, so let's do it! Al and Pat, Mike's going to need all the help you and your people can give him in assembly and processing so give him top priority on anything he needs. Let's see—how about your report, Mary?"

And so the meeting goes, with Tom astutely keeping the discussion on course, seeking individual commitments, discouraging tendencies of one person to throw darts at another, and specifically delineating opportunities for mutually supportive interactions.

"Earlier this morning I had a call from Pete. He called specifically to thank us for our outstanding performance last month. He's delighted with the improvement he's seeing, and he really sounded upbeat about the way the company is doing overall. I certainly want to echo his comments and add my own congratulations. I appreciate all the effort you all have been putting in, and I'm excited about the bottom-line evidence of how your efforts are paying off!"

Tom lingers with Frank after the meeting to discuss the appropriateness of Frank working closer with Mike on the tardiness issue. He also asks Frank how Mike might feel about being unnecessarily criticized in front of others.

When he leaves the conference room, Tom heads to his office, speaking to several people along the way. He greets Tammy again, steps into his own office to drop his notes on his desk, turns to leave again, and says,

"I'm headed to lunch at the Green Garden with Chuck. Is there anything you need before I go?"

"I guess not," Tammy replies, appreciative of the way Tom so considerately keeps her informed.

After lunch Tom gets a call from Alice, the manager of administration. She seems a little upset and asks if she may see him. Tom volunteers to drop in at her office.

"Hi, Alice. What's up?"

"Well, I hate to complain, but we're having a terrible time with the salesmen doing an incomplete job of documenting their expense reports. Sam just doesn't seem to convey to them the need to follow the policy on expense reimbursement. You remember that, as you suggested, we even had him involved in our redesign of the form so it could be as simple as possible to use. The problem is so bad I almost brought it up at the meeting this morning; then when I got back, I found this stack of garbage reports on my desk from today's mail!"

"You're right that our policies and procedures have been developed for a purpose, Alice, and they need to be followed or modified, if necessary, so they can be followed effectively. But have you talked with Sam about this?"

"Not recently . . . but he knew what a problem we were having when we redesigned the form for him. I assumed he would hop on the problem with us once the new form was ready."

"Well, why don't you talk with Sam about it. He may also have assumed the new form and simplified instructions would do the trick by themselves, but I'm sure he will work on his people if need be. Should the three of us meet, or do you want to pursue it with him first?"

"Ummmm . . . let me talk to him and I'll get back to you if we need you."

Later in the afternoon Tammy reminds Tom that he had wanted to speak with Larry Moneybags, the president of a financial organization, about the status of plans for a possible joint venture to handle equipment leasing.

"Oh, that's right. Thanks. Would you get him on the line, or give me his number?" Tom asks as he glances over his notes on the last conversation he had with Larry."

"He's on line one."

"Hi, Larry. How are you doing? . . . Oh, I understand. Well, I knew you wanted to talk to me soon, and since I'm going to be out of town for the next two days, I just thought I'd check with you. I'll be back in the office Friday, but if you need to reach me in the meantime, I'll be at the Anatole Hotel in Dallas."

Tammy has stayed a little late to be sure Tom has everything he needs for tomorrow's trip. They briefly discuss several special items for her to attend to in his absence and they then stroll out to the parking area and to their cars. As they part, Tom thanks her again for her help, and she wishes him a safe trip.

As he heads for home Tom smiles inwardly about the way the day has gone. He's proud of the way the group is improving, and the way they seem to be learning to work together better. Frustratingly slowly, he thinks, but there is a hint of a smile as he reminds himself that they are committed to improvement—and they are getting there!

He hasn't driven very far before his thoughts shift to his wife and children, and how nice it is going to be to have a relaxed evening together!

Throughout this day Tom has been living by the guidelines summarized as the "Ten Commandments for Good Interpersonal Relationships."

Ten Commandments for
Good Interpersonal Relationships

1. Be friendly and cheerful. Be positive in your interactions. Look for brighter sides of everything, and don't unnecessarily burden others with your problems or negative outlook. It has been said it takes 72 muscles to frown and only 14 to smile.

2. Speak less than you listen. Remember that you have two ears and one mouth and use them accordingly. Ask questions and listen—*really* listen!

3. Maintain a calm manner, remembering that the way you say something is more significant than what you say. When your nonverbal messages are in conflict with the verbals, the nonverbals will prevail.

4. Keep an open mind and avoid defensiveness. Practice disagreeing without being disagreeable. Seek mutual understanding, not a "victory" based on argumentation and conflict.

5. Maintain a balance between constructive criticism and praise. When giving guidance, be sure it is constructive. Watch for opportunities to give sincere praise—and give it.

6. Remember that it is amazing what you can get done when you don't care who gets the credit. Avoid bragging, which tends to provide superficial and short-term gratification. You will feel much better if people learn from others, or from your behavior, about your strengths and weaknesses.

7. Keep others informed in a positive way. Share insights into potential challenges and opportunities—but avoid promises. When you do make commitments, be dependable.

8. Avoid gossip, negative comments about others, and the spreading of rumors. Live so that others' disparaging comments about you won't be believed. Don't support or

participate in unconstructive griping sessions behind the backs of others.

9. Be sensitive and considerate regarding the limitations, feelings, and anxieties of others. Don't succumb to opportunities for humor at the expense of others. Be compassionate and give support freely during their times of need. Be patient and understanding.

10. Hold others in high esteem. Appreciate others as real live human beings with personal feelings, including their needs for self-esteem and recognition. Be interested in their thoughts, their circumstances, their families, and their futures.

Chapter 11

Teamwork Means Working Together— As in "CO . . ."

We are born for cooperation, as are the feet, the hands, the eye-lids, and the upper and lower jaws.

Marcus Aurelius

Perhaps one of the best ways to examine what teamwork is all about is to recognize that it is a matter of people doing things *together,* and to review some of the wonderful togetherness words that begin with "CO . . ." The three most fundamentally useful words are COmmunication, COordination, and COoperation.

COmmunication

Since mutual understanding of a group's goal is essential to its effective and efficient functioning, communication among its members is one of the most important aspects of exemplary teamwork. What is our goal? How can we get there? Which alternatives best fit our needs and circumstances? When should various benchmarks be passed, and when should we be finished? Who needs to perform what elements, and who needs to help or be helped by whom? Clearly, our ability to discuss and understand these matters will depend on our communication, as will our ability to remain abreast of progress, shortfalls, and the need for revised objectives and strategies.

COordination

Given the elements of what needs to happen and who is available and responsible to make it happen, there is a fundamental need to coordinate interactions, just as the gears in a watch must be properly coordinated for it to keep the right time. When I finish what I need to do, how should I plan, most conveniently and correctly, to turn it over to you for your contribution? Would it help you if we turned over some of what we've done before we've done it all? If things go better or worse than planned, who should we tell? And if we get in trouble, who will most likely be able to help us out? Would it help you in your efforts if we modify the way we pursue our objectives?

COoperation

Regardless of how well we understand our objectives and commitments, and regardless of how well we have mapped out how we can optimally coordinate our efforts, teamwork cannot be maximized unless we function in a cooperative atmosphere or with a spirit of mutual support and assistance. How important to me are your challenges relative to my own? How concerned am I about your success as an associate, both now and in the future? Am I willing to go out of my way to help you learn and perform? Am I even willing to suffer some setbacks in my own progress to help you achieve significant accomplishments that on balance will result in a higher level of success for our overall mission?

There are numerous additional "CO" words that are appropriate to or descriptive of good teamwork. In some, the first two letters are root prefixes. In others, the fact that they start with "co" is simply a coincidence of spelling. Neverthe-less, they are well suited to describe how outstanding team-mates interact.

Good team players tend to *contact* and *correspond* with each other. They *consult* or *confer* with others, engaging in enough *conversation* to allow themselves to *consider* alter-nate points of view, to *contribute* their own ideas, and even to *confide* in others regarding their apprehensions and anxi-eties. They welcome opportunities to *comingle* suggestions and to *consolidate* them into *concurrent* strategies and *corre-lated* action plans around which the participants can *coalesce* with both individual and *collective commitment.*

In working together, some may occasionally have to *con-sent* to solutions other than their own, but at worst, they will *coexist* with the most positive relationship possible. They will work in *concert* to ensure their individual objectives will *coincide* with the purpose of the organization. They will *co-author* and *co-execute* plans and strategies that will optimally utilize resources in pursuit of their *collective* and *congruent* goals. As they *commence* to pursue *components* of their *com-mon* and *comprehensive* endeavors they will *convene* when-ever necessary to *confirm* that they are *converging* on their objectives in *concordance* with sound business principles.

Good team players will seek and maintain *cohesiveness* more than just *consensus.* They will seek ways to *complement* each other with their unique strengths and needs and to *compliment* all involved as they make progress. They will recognize that they may never be fully *compatible* and *conge-nial* with some team members, but they can always be at least *considerate.* They will *commend* others for opportunities, *congratulating* them when they succeed. They will similarly be *concerned* and *conciliatory* during times of stress, being guided by *compassion* and offering *comfort* and *condolences* as needed.

Following in the spirit of the preceding paragraphs, indi-viduals will see themselves not just as members of a group, but more likely as *cohorts, colleagues,* and *compatriots.* They will welcome opportunities to assist associates in other groups in *committees*. They will view themselves as a *coalition* or *consortium*, and they will *counsel* freely with their associates in *councils, congregations, conferences* and *congresses*. Their *companies* and *corporations* will take pride in their *consonant* atmospheres.

And, hopefully, we will all enjoy improvements in our *communities* and in the wonderful *confederation* of these United States!

Chapter 12

Criteria for Evaluating Teamwork

> *Coming together is a beginning;*
> *keeping together is progress; and*
> *working together is success.*
>
> **Henry Ford**

*O*ne of my favorite stories about teamwork is about a sales manager who gathered his national sales force of twenty people together from all over the country. It was their annual sales meeting for reviewing the past year, looking ahead to the next year, training, and bolstering the group's morale. New products were introduced to the group, and toward the end of the conference, the manager took some time to introduce the new incentive compensation plan.

"As I mentioned yesterday, we have designed a new incentive compensation plan for next year. You each have been given a yellow sheet with a territory forecast tabulated, and at the bottom you will notice that there is a targeted dollar figure indicating the total sales volume we expect you to produce. Does everyone see your targeted amount? Any questions?

"O.K. Here's how the incentive program is going to work. We're going to rank all of you according to the percentage of sales you actually produce above your targeted amount. The person who produces the highest percentage above standard will win a new car not to exceed $20,000 in value. The second winner will receive a $5,000 cash bonus. Seventeen of you will be able to keep your jobs as long as you produce at least as much volume as we've asked for in your territory. That brings us to the lowest producer in terms of percentage attainment of your territory standard."

There was a pause, then the sales manager said, "Whoever is the lowest producer at the end of the year will be fired! . . . Oh, by the way, I *do* hope you will all cooperate with each other a lot better next year than you did this last year!"

So much for his inspirational message on teamwork!

I have no idea where this case originated. In fact, perhaps it isn't even true. It could be, though, because it is entirely consistent with our propensity in business to focus almost exclusively on results (content) and to a very limited extent on relationships (process).

Then there's a story of a company that had a chance, the executive committee believed, to increase sales astronomically in one year. As they reviewed this exciting outlook, the executives agreed unanimously that they really might achieve their incredible projection, but only if the seven key people directly below the executive committee would work together in a *highly* cooperative way. After further discussion, the top executives agreed that they themselves could control the profitability that could accompany the higher volume of sales, and they kept coming back to the fundamental need for a cooperative effort among the seven key managers to reach the volume target. As they reviewed the enormous profit that would accompany the attainment of the desired growth and reminded each other of the extremely important target of increased market share and customer satisfaction in a lucrative marketplace, they decided to set aside a bonus pool that would accumulate about $100,000 for distribution to the seven key managers.

After the executive committee meeting, the president sought evaluation of the bonus plan. The executive committee was thinking of distributing the bonus pool to the participants on the basis of their individual contributions. This was to be another variation on the tradition in which individual results might be measured, hence pursued, at the expense of the effectiveness of the group. After evaluation it became clear that individual departments could fulfill their narrowly defined functions well enough to reinforce the phenomenal increase desired, though there was repeated discussion of the challenge being the outstanding level of communication and cooperation which would be required of the "super seven."

Consideration was given to three ways in which the earmarked bonus pool could be distributed. First, it could be distributed according to the individual contributions of each of the seven people. Second, it could be distributed in proportion to their base pay levels. Third, the distribution could simply be equal, with one seventh of the pool going to each.

The first approach, we concluded, could be setting the stage for each key person to focus not just on the attainment of the targeted growth, but also on ways to favorably influence the perceptions of others as to his or her *individual contribution* to the successful attainment of the growth goal. As he understood the situation, the president concluded this approach might indeed be risky.

We also concluded that the teamwork efforts needed, and which might actually be expended by the bonus participants, might be completely unrelated to their base pay levels. The second approach could have resulted in a bonus for a terrific team player with a lower base salary being smaller than the bonus for a mediocre team player with a higher base salary. This approach, therefore, was discarded because it did not have a clear, logical fit regarding focused reinforcement of teamwork.

The discussion kept leading us back to teamwork being the key to the achievement of this challenging objective. So, to keep the seven individuals clearly focused as a team, the decision went to the third alternative—equal shares for each if the team succeeded in its mission.

There are two postscripts to this story. First, the team functioned outstandingly well together, and the extraordinary actual growth was well above the target that was needed to trigger the bonus payments. Second, the success of this team was enhanced by a well thought-out plan. Clear understandings were developed based on the specific goals and unique conditions that were reviewed. This success story should not be extrapolated to suggest that group bonuses are a cure-all. As was done in this case, each situation deserves its own analysis and carefully considered strategy.

A highly respected colleague, Dr. Herman Gadon, and I have had an opportunity to work with a very progressive organization to study and revise their performance review and compensation plans. This has been a particularly productive and pleasant assignment because it was commissioned at the request of a dynamic and progressive chief executive officer, and it has included the active involvement of several dozen key people who, as potential users of our proposals, have been very important and helpful contributors to our work.

At the outset of our work, we examined the performance evaluation forms that were being used. They included criteria typically found on performance review forms such as work quality, work quantity, job knowledge, judgment, and initiative. During one of our work sessions, someone observed that though the company takes great pride in its progressiveness and in the promotion of teamwork and constructive relationships, none of the performance review forms sought comments evaluating teamwork. To fill the void, we (all of us working on the project) wrote and rewrote some descriptions that could be used to represent various levels or qualities of teamwork. The objective was to be broadly descriptive yet concise. The following definitions, resulting from the group's efforts, have been incorporated into the company's performance review forms.

Descriptions of Teamwork Levels

- **Outstanding:** Consistently offers aid and is always available to help others. Extremely courteous, well mannered, and polite. Always considers the needs, interests, comfort, and ease of others.

- **Above Expectations:** Can usually be counted on to help. Very aware of others' feelings and rights. Conscientious about team involvement. Always polite. Often offers assistance.
- **Expected:** Generally cooperative on the job. Observes common courtesies; does not offend.
- **Below Expectations:** Too often uncooperative when faced with reasonable requests for assistance. Occasionally impolite to co-workers or others.
- **Unacceptable:** A "roadblock" to co-workers, customers, or suppliers. Frequently rude. Causes noticeable discomfort to others. Usually uncooperative.

Chapter 13

Recruiting and Selecting Effective Team Players

*You can pick lemons off trees, but
you have to dig for diamonds.*

Proverb

When John D. Rockefeller was asked to what he owed his success he said, "Others!" Andrew Carnegie gave similar credit when he said, "Take away my factories, take away my money, but leave me my men and I'll soon have my factories and money again." And Ray Kroc observed, "You're only as good as the people you hire."

What about these thoughts by Rockefeller, Carnegie, and Kroc? Were they correct in giving so much credit to their associates? And if associates are so important, what sort of guidelines should we use regarding the best types of people to seek? One set of criteria could be:

- bright
- knowledgeable
- exhibiting good judgement
- analytic
- creative
- innovative, and
- energetic.

Not a bad set of traits! And, in fact, a person having these traits might very likely make a good impression on an interviewer. But before we conclude that a candidate with these traits should be offered a job, we need to consider several other things.

First, when people who are hired don't work out, it generally follows that the person didn't fit in or was ineffective in the way he or she interacted with others, be they associates or customers. Much less often it is because the person did not have the ability needed. In other words, mistakes most often tend to be made on *will do* factors, not *can do* factors.

Second, in view of this first point, we need to ask what is known about this apparently marvelous candidate's will-do nature. Among the positive traits listed previously for the candidate, there is no indication that he or she also has traits that will contribute to his or her success in dealing with others. Maybe the candidate will fit in well, but we won't know unless we can get a feel for the extent to which the candidate is:

- sensitive to the needs of others
- understanding as a listener
- concerned about communications
- willing to share credit
- respectful of others
- an advocate of teamwork

Until we have judged the candidate on these additional factors, we don't really have all the information we should to make an intelligent hiring decision.

There are those who haven't considered how important it is to evaluate how candidates might interact with their would-be associates, even after making mistake after mistake by hiring people who can't or don't get along. Others may have some interest in trying to predict potential interaction patterns, but don't quite know how to go about it. A third group sets themselves up for failure by hiring or promoting people who have admirable results-oriented skills even though they know in their hearts that the candidates are likely to be disruptive to the organization.

One company president hired a technical vice president based on the candidate's knowledge and experience—even though there was ample evidence in the reference checks that the individual would in all likelihood not get along well with his associates. Soon after the new vice president reported to work, he began taking credit for anything good in which he was even remotely involved. At the same time, he distanced himself from problem areas until they began to turn around. He aggressively stifled any disclosures of bad news by his subordinates, thereby inhibiting problems from surfacing so they might be addressed and solved. He even began manipulating data to make himself look good in the eyes of his supervisor. In short, this key executive placed his perceived self-interest far above the good of anyone else and of the organization for which he was working.

In spite of serious conflicts between this vice president and others, and in particular between him and the senior vice president to whom he reported, the president promoted him to peer status with his former supervisor. Reinforced by this vote of confidence by the president, the self-serving executive became more aggressive in his efforts to enhance his own image and degrade the images of others. It took a near mutiny throughout the organization to bring this mistake in hiring to a much-too-late resolution through the removal of the antagonist.

The president admitted he'd been captivated by the candidate's superficial poise and charm and by his ability to present his technical potential in extremely impressive ways. The president further explained that he compounded his mistake by promoting the problematic executive to report directly to him with the wishful thought that he, as president, could personally guide Mr. Difficult to improved behavior. He again admitted, though, that this effort to save the vice president was made because of the halo effect of the vice president's technical skill and potential. Unfortunately the salvage effort was destined to fail not only because the vice president caused such serious problems, but also because the president realized too late that principled relationships are at least as important as expedient results.

This is not an isolated case. One of the most common mistakes made in hiring or promoting decisions is to place far too much emphasis on a prospect's technical skills, and not enough on the person's process- or relationship-building skills.

A similarly tragic story probably was narrowly avoided by a company owner when, recognizing that he frequently made common mistakes in recruiting and selecting, he solicited help in hiring a new key executive. The candidate and hiring executive both were marketers, and in their initial conversations, they apparently had dazzled each other with their positive and upbeat conversation. The advisor immediately pointed out that the resume implied that the candidate had held four jobs, yet it gave no dates for any of them. In subsequent conversation, it became clear that the prospective marketer had grouped his prior jobs into four categories in an attempt to defocus from his employment record of hopping in and out of twenty-two jobs in twenty-one years!

There were other key points that suggested this candidate was not prepared to meet the company owner's needs. In addition to not holding any job as long as two years, he was unable to express *anything* positive about *any* of his former supervisors. Certainly, it is possible that he had suffered a rare streak of bad luck in choosing his supervisors, but it is statistically unlikely.

When asked about his perceived strengths and weaknesses ("What have you done to improve your own strengths or abilities during the last year or two?"), he responded that he'd recently elected to spend at least fifteen minutes a day with his children so that *he* could become a more well-rounded individual. How could an individual make a more self-centered statement? As you certainly would suspect, the decision was made to reject the applicant.

Though the decision to reject a candidate is not necessarily a clear-cut decision, the odds are that this candidate would have been a "below expectations" performer on the company's teamwork scale.

Since hiring mistakes are seldom a matter of seriously misjudging the candidate's technical skills, shouldn't we increase the consideration placed on process and relationship issues?

Helpful Hints on Hiring Harmonious Help

1. Anticipate future human resource needs so you can more carefully recruit and select candidates.
2. Recruit continuously by watching for outstanding people who live and work around you.
3. More precisely define both the characteristics and the capabilities of people who will be likely to succeed.
4. Place your recruiting and selecting endeavors high among your priorities.
5. Discipline yourself to rise above temptations to take short cuts or to accept compromise.
6. Seek successful prospects, which generally means candidates who are currently employed.
7. Give ample consideration to existing employees who might qualify for promotion into a vacancy.
8. Be courteous to all candidates at all stages in the selection process.
9. Efficiently sift down the candidate pool to a small group of finalists through resume reviews and preliminary telephone or personal screening interviews.
10. Conduct probing in-depth interviews with the use of open-ended questions.
11. Be alert to your personal biases which tend to get in the way of professional objectivity.
12. Probe beyond discussions of what candidates have done into why and how they did it.
13. Maintain good rapport during each interview to encourage information to flow freely from the interviewee.
14. Keep an open mind while gathering bits and pieces of information until patterns become evident.

15. Interpret various patterns discerned in terms of how a candidate might behave in the future.
16. Listen five to ten times more than you talk, and keep the interview on a purposeful course.
17. Focus initially on learning about the candidate, postponing the urge to tell about the company and the opportunity.
18. Gather others' opinions through the use of multiple sequential (but generally not *gang*) interviews.
19. Do persist in your efforts to obtain telephone reference checks with former associates.
20. Begin focusing on potential goals for the candidate during the late stages of the selection process and continue into the induction and operation stages of employment.

Promoting Existing Employees

Most of these guidelines on hiring new employees also apply to promoting existing employees. We have an opportunity to review much better information when we are making selection decisions pertaining to promotions than we do when deciding on potential new employees. But again we see our propensity to focus on task-oriented results (or potential results) substantially more than we focus on relationship building (or the potential for the building of relationships).

According to the Peter Principle, we tend to promote people to their level of incompetence. The fact is that the higher one rises in an organization, the more important his or her skills at communicating, coordinating, and cooperating will become. Yet we continue to promote the best salesperson to branch manager, the best accountant to office manager, the best machinist to foreman, and the best physicist to department manager. In so doing we often lose a top-flight producer and gain a mediocre or poor supervisor. It's not that the best producer *can't* be the best choice for promotion, it's just that other factors also should be considered. And when our choice is made, almost certainly the promotee deserves more preparation and guidance than he or she is likely to get.

As one executive once jokingly commented, "How do we make a supervisor? We change the color of the badge!"

The producer may spend *years* in learning and practicing task details in his or her profession, but only minutes, hours, days, or weeks in becoming oriented to the ways of leadership and relationships. Interestingly, John D. Rockefeller noted, "The ability to deal with people is as purchasable a commodity as sugar or coffee. And I pay more for that ability than any other under the sun."

The irony of the lack of attention to selecting and training of people with regard to their skills in relationships is that tasks usually involve facts and straightforward, highly predictable principles. Relationships, on the other hand, involve people, and it is people who are challenging because each is unique, complex, and not entirely predictable!

As Scott Porter says, "Leadership would be easy if it weren't for people." But *people* are the heart of our challenge. They are the essence of our success or failure! They are the resources to which almost all managers should devote higher levels of attention—not just for the purpose of "being nice," but for cultivating talent and teamwork, enhancing individual and collective performance, and ultimately, improving results.

Once the decision has been made to hire or to promote from within, appropriate guidance should be given to the individual at the outset of his or her new assignment. This process, called inducting, is covered in the next chapter.

Chapter 14

Welcoming the New Member of the Squad

You can buy someone's time, you can buy someone's physical presence at a given place; you can even buy a measured number of skilled muscular motions per hour or day. But you cannot buy enthusiasm; you cannot buy initiative; you cannot buy loyalty; you cannot buy devotion of hearts, minds, and souls. You have to earn these things.

Clarence Francis

Like individuals, an organization has only one chance to make a good first impression. Even small efforts can work wonders in alleviating new-kid-on-the-block anxieties and to constructively begin helping newcomers through the complex transition from outsider to insider.

Once at a large corporate headquarters, I saw a familiar executive wandering aimlessly in a hallway. He was an outstanding individual to whom my client and I had devoted substantial recruitment and selection attention. In greeting him, I commented that I didn't realize he would be joining the firm so soon; in a somewhat disappointed tone, he replied that apparently his new boss didn't realize it either! He was attempting to begin a new phase of his career under a new supervisor who had left town without even demonstrating sensitivity enough to leave instructions for the new man. It was a needlessly unpleasant, and all-too-common first experience for the newcomer.

We have all had good and not-so-good experiences in breaking into a new group. The way we were treated probably made a significant impact on how soon, and to what extent, we became useful members in the class, neighborhood, volunteer group, in-law family, or employer's organization. Considerate team members recognize the importance of integrative transitions for new members and will go out of their way to welcome and assist new associates. Less considerate group members will tend to maintain barriers to the intrusion of others into their comfortable cliques.

Years ago I arrived at Alamogordo, New Mexico, to speak at a statewide convention. I'll never forget what a pleasant experience that was, primarily because of the warmth of my reception. The hotel staff were collectively the most pleasant group of hotel employees I've ever met. But what stands out most in my memory was the way the convention officers welcomed me.

As usual, I arrived early to be comfortably certain of being available and rested when I was scheduled to speak. After checking into the hotel, I headed toward the convention reception and registration area. Only a few others, mostly organization officers, had arrived as early as I had, and I noticed about a half-dozen of them talking as they stood in a circle near the registration desk. Rather than ignoring me and leaving me to fend for myself, this group opened as they saw me approach. They greeted me warmly, introduced themselves, and proceeded to integrate me into their conversation as if I were another officer who had known them for years. Throughout my stay these people never left me standing alone; they frequently asked if there was anything I needed or if they could help me. By the time I left, I felt as if the entire convention had been set up just so I would have an opportunity to meet so many new friends!

Now think about how you were received the last time you joined an organization. Were you one of the main centers of attention until you felt like an integral part of the group, or did you just feel that you at least didn't seem to be getting in anybody's way as they continued their own long-term friendships? How long was it before you had personally met all the members? And have you now become part of one of the cliques within the organization, or do you and most of the other members sit at different tables with different people at the periodic meetings? Even in service organizations (formed to develop camaraderie during the pursuit of worthy service projects), members usually find it more convenient and comfortable to gravitate into their own little subgroups. Those wishing to encourage broader orientation and involvement in activities of the club should begin by welcoming newcomers and allocating high priority to total group cohesiveness.

In our task-oriented environments, the natural tendencies of newcomers often work counter to their early acceptance into a group and the effective development of team relationships. One company, in dire need of better manufacturing engineering efforts, hired a brilliant, experienced, and creative—but insensitive—manager for the manufacturing engineering department. When he reported to work, he set out to prove his brilliance and potential worth to the organization. Within hours, he pointed out everything he felt was wrong, and in so doing, he was equally successful at criticizing and insulting virtually everyone except his immediate supervisor! Halfway through his first afternoon, he had written a memo to all the engineers in his department beginning with the words "Henceforth you shall not. . . ." What a beginning! And, in fact, the end was not long in coming. The manufacturing manager quickly offended so many people that he was discharged before he had time to become the hero he wished he could be. He lost his job, and the organization lost a potentially valuable resource.

Perhaps supervisory guidance at the very beginning of the first day could have prevented this occurrence. Supervisors should coach new associates that understanding the organization and gaining acceptance by their other associates are among the first orders of business. No one is without risk of future mistakes. And when mistakes are made or help is needed, those who have become accepted will find their fellow team members rallying to their assistance.

In their book, *Fitting In,* Dr. Natasha Josefowitz and Dr. Herman Gadon extensively discuss how group membership evolves and how difficult it may be for a newcomer to become accepted as a full-fledged member. They point out that "acceptance has to be earned; it is not just given." They also indicate: "Most of us want to belong—to be part of a group. We need to be accepted. We want to be liked, respected, paid attention to, even loved. We want to be heard as well as seen, and we want to fit in."

Josefowitz and Gadon have identified four stages of fitting in. Initially there is "exclusion" or ". . . nonacceptance of the newcomer, usually out of neglect." Next there is the "undesirable assignments" stage. "This stage is known as paying your dues. The new person goes from outsider to lowest person on the totem pole. . . . In other words, you are not kept apart any more, but you are the person with the lowest status and you are on probation." Stage three is "hazing," commonplace in fraternities, the military, and among sports teams, but also evident in other groups such as office departments or work crews. During this stage, senior group members may flaunt their positions by pushing or teasing newcomers.

It isn't until the fourth stage that a newcomer becomes a member. Josefowitz and Gadon call it "incorporation: earning your stripes; becoming a member." In making this transition, the new person will leave behind such labels as recruit, apprentice, trainee, greenhorn, etc. He or she now has arrived in the inner circle and likely will in turn participate in the challenging and hazing of future fledglings.

Supervisors can do a great deal to assist newcomers as they move through these four stages of acceptance. Unfortunately, however, as these authors point out, "Our studies indicate that employers give remarkably low priority to the need for orienting new workers. Employers assign very little in time, budget, and personnel to the task." The following list cites 10 steps a supervisor can take to facilitate the transition of a newcomer, to minimize the anxiety or discomfort he or she may experience, and to hasten his or her achievement of high levels of productivity.

What a tremendous opportunity we have to improve the ways we go about welcoming new associates. And what a significant number of opportunities there are each year to put improvements into effect. As Josefowitz and Gadon point out, "We are a society on the move. Each year, on the average, 20 million Americans, or one out of five people who are working, change jobs, and another six million enter the labor force. Therefore, on every work day 100,000 people experience their first day on the job."

Surely the induction of our human resources is a challenge worthy of more attention!

SUPERVISORS' GUIDE FOR INDUCTING NEWCOMERS

1. Clarify the organization's goals and your expectations regarding hours, resources, performance, and results.
2. Be sure the newcomer understands the importance of becoming accepted initially and building teamwork continuously.
3. Reintroduce the newcomer to people who were met during the employment screening process, and include introductions to others with whom interaction is likely.
4. Provide a clear understanding of policies, procedures (formal or informal), codes of conduct, and standards of ethics that will be expected for the person to function properly.
5. Discuss such basics as the organization structure, the company's physical facilities, locations of restrooms, and lunch or break areas and their use.
6. Review the manner in which the employee will be paid, overtime rules, bonus or incentive plans, elements of the benefit package and payroll deduction items.
7. Whenever possible, support your comments with copies of employee handbooks, policy and procedure manuals, a letter or memo welcoming your associate, and other useful background or reference documents.
8. Check more frequently than you might think necessary regarding any questions or requests for help that the newcomer may have.
9. Take every legitimate opportunity to reinforce early progress on either task or relationship matters as you observe or hear of things being done well.
10. Above all, take the time to handle these steps well. You are making a sound investment, not just for the individual, but for the team!

Chapter **15**

Delegating to Strengthen Teams and Improve Morale

*The best executive is the one who has
the sense to pick good people and
self-restraint enough to keep from
meddling while they perform.*

Theodore Roosevelt

Good people need to be challenged. At the end of the day they want to feel good about having done something worthwhile. They need to have a chance to achieve and to be recognized for achievement. Furthermore, the brighter and more dedicated they are, the more they need to perceive at least some sense of control over their own work situation.

Stress research has shown that when people feel they have at least some control over their work situations, their blood pressures will rise temporarily when they face a challenge, but will subside rapidly. When they lack control or perceive that they do, people *remain* stressed, and, among other symptoms, they are likely to interact discourteously with customers and associates.

In the absence of good delegating practices by their immediate supervisors, subordinates at any level of an organization are destined to be underutilized, frustrated, probably bored, and certainly less enthusiastic and effective than they could be. They are likely to view themselves simply as pawns, and they will feel more like outsiders than insiders. By contrast, when authority and responsibility have been delegated to them, they will have greater chances to achieve. They will be provided opportunities to stretch and flex their intellectual and professional muscles. And they will rightfully view themselves as being worthy of responsibility and as having worthwhile input. They will enjoy the added ability to be able to significantly influence, if not control, their professional destinies. And in short, they will see themselves as respected members of the supervisor's team! We are so prone to think of teamwork as strictly a matter of lateral relationships that it is easy to lose sight of the tremendous teamwork implications regarding supervisor-subordinate relationships.

Delegation by the next level up is not only beneficial to the "delegatees," but is also necessary for the full effectiveness and efficiency of the "delegator." Only through sound delegation can the president devote his or her time to matters of the presidency, and vice presidents to high-level decisions requiring their attention, and so on down the organization. Those who delegate effectively will mitigate problems associated with getting bogged down in details, and they are likely to be both ready and available to respond to unforeseen challenges or emergencies requiring attention at their level. Effective delegators also will have more time to devote attention to their roles as communicators and coordinators as well as to demonstrate and encourage high levels of cooperative spirit.

It is interesting that in most situations lacking in delegation, the would-be delegator is likely to voice a desire for his or her subordinates to be willing to accept more authority and responsibility while the subordinates are simultaneously saying that they wish their supervisor would yield more authority and responsibility to them!

Frequently we find that a supervisor's reluctance to delegate stems from his or her concern that the subordinates already are busy even to the point, perhaps, of being overloaded. The effective executive will not let this concern stand in the way of delegation. All appropriate authority and responsibility must be pushed to lower levels in the hierarchy. If need be, those at the lower levels should be taught and coached in turn to delegate everything appropriate to even lower levels in the hierarchy. This process should continue until there are enough people at the operating level to handle all that needs to be handled at that level. And there should be enough supervisors to handle appropriate responsibilities at their level so the managers can do their jobs, directors can do their jobs, vice presidents can do theirs, and the president can do his or hers. Deterioration in this area cannot be allowed if the team is to function at its full potential.

A spirit of commitment to this concept is essential. It is easy to outline the steps that can be taken to improve delegation, and they are not difficult to understand. But they will serve no purpose if the potential delegator is blocked from implementing them because of an inappropriate sense of guilt.

I was thrilled by involvement in the almost instantaneous improvement in the delegation skills of the president of an insurance company. He succinctly explained a turnaround in delegating ability by saying, "I used to think of delegating as 'dumping' on my employees, but now I understand it as giving them a chance to grow!" This is a fundamental philosophical issue that impacts a manager's effectiveness in the art of delegation.

A second philosophical issue concerns the recognition that, by delegating authority and responsibility down the ladder, the delegator cannot relieve himself or herself of accountability. The delegator who does not feel residual accountability and make provisions to follow up has *abdicated*, not delegated. He or she must select and prepare associates for acceptance of expanded authority and responsibility and should, as an important part of the delegation process, agree from the start on the manner and timing of follow-up steps. That way, the delegator will be properly informed of the status of whatever has been delegated.

This brings us to a third philosophical issue. When good delegation practices are not in effect, there is a tendency to put *all* the blame on the delegator—which is not quite fair. The third fundamental philosophical issue involves recognizing that delegation is a complex, often emotional process involving two or more people, each with different abilities, insights, levels of confidence, anxieties, and habits. If they are to succeed in this special aspect of teamwork called delegation, they must appropriately communicate, coordinate, and cooperate during the period of transition.

First, let us examine the emotional needs of the delegator. When performing a task himself or herself, he or she has excellent information at all times regarding the status of the task. Whether the task is on course or not a level of comfort comes with that knowledge. When it comes time to delegate, though, the delegator will not only be giving up what might be a favorite activity, but will also be losing the automatic awareness of the task's status. It is this loss of constant awareness that may make the delegator nervous and all too often, leads the delegator to check on the delegatee prematurely (or at least prematurely in the eyes of the delegatee). At its worst, this nervousness may even lead the delegator to retrieve the assignment and complete it alone.

How about the feelings of the delegatee? Perhaps there will be a little anxiety about whether he or she is really up to the task. This issue can be addressed and probably alleviated by the delegator's clear delineation of the desired result, the deadline, and the genuine assurance that the delegator will be available for help and guidance as needed.

Suppose you are the delegator and I am the delegatee. Now that you have demonstrated confidence in me and I have accepted the challenge, more likely than not I will want to prove to you that I am worthy of this opportunity. This feeling, mixed with a normal amount of pride, is likely to cause me to want to go off on my own, complete the assignment, and deliver it to you all wrapped up like a nice, little package. In other words, my natural tendency probably will be to avoid bothering you—and, hence, maybe even avoid contacting you—until I'm done.

Note the predictable situation this will put us in. You as the delegator will be nervous in the absence of information, so your need is for *more* information flowing between us than people might normally expect. On the other hand, my interest is to perform admirably, providing you with *less* information along the way than might normally be expected—and certainly far less information than you would like! These diametric positions leave us with a real teamwork challenge. It is essential, therefore, that we discuss at the outset how we can most effectively handle the passing of the baton. Both parties need to understand that the transition may be complex, and that each should be dedicated to being sensitive to each other's needs. As an integral part of the agreement, both parties need to reach an understanding as to how frequently they should touch base, when these status reviews should occur, and what form they should take. A mutually considerate approach doesn't have to be difficult: it just needs to be understood and followed!

There is a fourth and final philosophical consideration. Delegators should learn to accept the facts that (a) nothing is perfect, and (b) everything is different—including ways to accomplish an objective. Delegation conversations, therefore, should focus on the expected end result, major policy ground rules, and intermediate checkpoint provisions. In general, detailed matters on exactly how to accomplish the task should be left to the delegatee—preferably the first time around, but certainly on subsequent occasions. Otherwise, the delegator will be exhibiting a lack of confidence and may likely cause the delegatee to feel insulted. The experienced successful delegator will minimize any risk by appropriately negotiated intermediate checkpoints and by astutely remaining available for help without getting in the way. And the delegator will allow enough room for the delegatee to perform professionally and effectively. As General George S. Patton suggested, "Don't tell people how to do things. Discuss what the end result should be and they will then surprise you with their ingenuity."

Delegation:
Four Fundamental Philosophical Considerations

1. By properly delegating challenging assignments and opportunities to subordinates, a delegator will not be "dumping" on them, but giving them a chance to grow.
2. A delegator ultimately retains accountability for proper results. A would-be delegator who tries to avoid accountability will be *abdicating*, not *delegating*.
3. Since the delegating process involves two or more people, it can be considered a special type of teamwork opportunity involving the communicating, coordinating, and cooperating challenges that make up all teamwork efforts.
4. Because nothing is perfect and everything is different (including innumerable paths to outstanding results), delegation conversations should focus on end results expected, major ground rules, and intermediate checkpoints, not on trivial matters regarding approaches to be used.

How to Delegate—Some Guidelines

1. Analyze and clarify the goals of your organization.
2. Identify the elements for which you are the only person (or the objectively logical one) to be responsible.
3. Assess the abilities of the people under you who are available for various leadership or operational roles.
4. Support, develop, train, coach, guide, and challenge each of these people so they will rise to their optimal levels of performance.
5. Build for the future on the "winners," and develop action plans for addressing all cases of mediocrity or incompetence.
6. Before doing *anything,* ask yourself if there is someone else who could possibly do it.
7. Discuss possible delegation opportunities with potential delegatees; agree on the scope or dimensions of the assignment; establish appropriate intermediate checkpoints and how they will serve to facilitate progress or status reviews; express the willingness and desire to be available for further coaching or guiding as needed; and develop the understanding that you as the delegator see the proper execution of the delegated assignment as a team effort that will call on relationship skills as well as task-achievement dedication.
8. Recognize that even though it may take someone else longer than you, and even though he or she might do it differently, what really matters is whether the result is essentially good—not necessarily perfect, but good! (How would you define "perfect" anyway, other than the way you would have done it yourself?)
9. When your people approach you with questions or challenges, supportively ask them for their own recommendations or solutions instead of expediently giving them quick definitive answers.

10. Add additional upper-level people cautiously, but as necessary, for a full level of professional support.
11. Use your best subordinates to lead special task forces and to serve in your shoes from time to time.

Chapter 16

Meetings as a Teamwork Tool

It is impossible for ideas to compete if no forum for their presentation is provided or available.

Thomas Mann

We have discussed teamwork as a matter of communicating, coordinating, and cooperating. One of the best ways to accomplish all three is through good, properly run meetings. Not sloppy meetings. Not ordinary meetings. But excellent meetings!

Although good meetings can help substantially in developing successful teamwork, they should not be viewed as a cure-all or as a substitute for other useful interactions. Even when meetings are properly planned and orchestrated, there will be a need for appropriate one-on-one conversations, memos or letters, and telephone calls.

As useful as they can be when they are well run, meetings often are so poorly orchestrated that they become the devil's most sinful time-wasting technique.

Meetings and Committees at Their Worst

The following comments outline all-too-apt descriptions of meetings and their results when they are conducted the way so many of them are.

- "The most effective committee has three people, two of whom are absent."
- "A committee consists of people sitting around talking about things they should be doing."
- "A committee usually is made up of the unfit selected by the unwilling to do the unnecessary."
- "A meeting is where the loneliness of thought is replaced by the togetherness of nothing."
- "The words 'dull meeting' are redundant."
- "Beige is the only color on which a committee can agree."
- "A circle is a straight line drawn by a committee."
- "A camel is a horse designed by a committee."
- "A great way to lose a war is to run it by committee." (Sir Winston Churchill)
- "God so loved the world he didn't send a committee."
- "God could not have made the world in a week if he had had to attend management meetings." (Harold Reasoner)

Meetings can most effectively be used as communication, coordination, and cooperation aids. They serve best those who use them to:

- improve understanding of team objectives,
- communicate challenges, strategies, and status,
- coordinate efforts and schedules; *and*
- encourage cooperation in spirit and in fact.

Meetings fail when participants take comfort in "group think," and when they develop habits of talking about things they should be doing. Many people mistakenly try to use meetings to solve problems, completely and in detail, rather than using meetings effectively and efficiently as outlined above.

In one high-tech company, key technical management people spend inordinate amounts of time in meetings. Most executives go from the parking lot not to their offices, but to meetings. As the day unfolds, they find themselves leaving one meeting before it is over to dash to another one, only to arrive after that one has started. All this time spent in meetings contributes to a high level of indirect cost to the company.

In spite of all the horror stories propagated by the misuse of meetings and committees, *they can be immensely successful when properly set up and conducted.* The following outlines on how to hold successful meetings will assist those wishing to improve their meeting skills.

Holding Successful Meetings—An Overview

1. Plan the meeting with care.
2. Communicate in advance with attendees.
3. Conduct the meeting as planned.
4. Follow up on action commitments.
5. Continually review meeting effectiveness and efficiency.

Plan the Meeting with Care

- Clarify the purpose for every meeting.
- Ask: Is there a better way to accomplish the goal?
- Select attendees and chairmen carefully.
- Schedule regular meetings, cancelling them when appropriate.
- Hold special meetings as needed.
- Select appropriate facilities and locations.
- Develop a "vital factor" agenda.

Communicate in Advance with Attendees
- Distribute an agenda.
- Outline starting and ending times.
- Outline any expected preparation.
- Cover mechanics (date, time, location, time allocations, attendees).
- Confirm that prompt attendance is expected.

Conduct the Meeting as Planned
- Start the meeting on time.
- Review the purpose, agenda, and any changes.
- Clarify relevant background and procedures.
- Review progress on prior goals or commitments. (Progress? Variances? Problems? Planned improvements?)
- Discuss each agenda item as briefly as appropriate.
- Clarify goals and action steps after each item. (What action? By whom? When?)
- Record brief, results-oriented minutes indicating these action commitments.
- Maintain dynamic participation (brisk pace, broad participation, constructive teamwork).
- Support the group process (listen, mediate, reinforce, facilitate).
- Stay on vital issues (discuss, summarize, decide and move on).
- Adjourn promptly following a review of action commitments.

Follow up on Action Commitments
- Distribute minutes promptly.
- Stimulate timely action with scheduled action steps.
- Periodically review progress on action commitments.

Continually Review Meeting Effectiveness and Efficiency
- During meetings, listen beyond the words and periodically assess what seems to be going on.

- Immediately after each meeting, ask yourself how well the meeting went and how it might have been better.
- Periodically (perhaps every fourth or fifth meeting), ask the regular participants to provide feedback and discuss *their* perceptions of how the meetings are going.
- Control the tendency for regular meetings to be perpetuated beyond their usefulness.

The usefulness of these guidelines should not be restricted to those who call meetings; they should be used by other participants as well. If a meeting does not seem to be fulfilling its purpose, participants need to contribute efforts toward improvement. The guidelines indicate characteristics of well-run meetings generally. As long as they are followed, the team benefits regardless of who drives adherence.

The guidelines are just that—guidelines. Certainly an emergency would not allow the production or pre-meeting distribution of a written agenda. However, many people have improved the effectiveness of their meetings by following these guidelines in spirit.

Reaching Championship Levels

Many management observers have suggested that many organizations survive (or "get along") *in spite of* themselves, not *because* of themselves. By covering the elements discussed in the prior section, organizations will tend to ensure viability, but not necessarily awesome success.

In this section we will look at additional techniques and distinguishing cultural and attitudinal aspects of organizations that excel consistently.

Chapter 17

How about Vendors and Customers on Your Team?

*All are but parts of one
stupendous whole.*

Alexander Pope

One broadly oriented client says, "'We' are our company and all of our customers and vendors, and we all need to function at our best as a team." Another calls this concept "strategic partnering."

Several years ago, in separate conversations with two different chief executive officers of similar competitive enterprises, I heard diametric views regarding make-versus-buy decisions in their corporations. One adamantly took the position that the secret to success is to make everything you possibly can within your organization. The other chief executive was equally forceful in stating that his company's success was largely attributable to the policy of buying almost everything they could from subcontractors. The first executive's logic was to produce his own parts and assemblies to control quality more tightly. The second felt that his company could more predictably control their costs and effect strategic partnering by negotiating prices with vendors.

Whatever an organization's strategy may be regarding make-versus-buy decisions, the key issue is the delivery of quality products or services at cost-effective prices and in a timely fashion. The measure of effectiveness is a customer base that consistently feels that expectations have been favorably satisfied (or exceeded) over the long term.

In one approach toward procurement, the buying organization not only seeks to buy wisely to get good value for the purchasing dollar, but also to chip away at the vendor's price continually, even to the extent that the vendor's ability to perform for the price is in jeopardy.

A more principled approach to sound customer-vendor relations over the long term involves commitments by separate and distinct organizations to work in concert for their mutual success. How? Through the same approach appropriate for sub-groups within any organization—teamwork. The formula for customer-vendor teamwork is the same as for interdepartmental (or any other) teamwork. It calls for everyone involved to commit to quality communication, coordination, and cooperation.

Relatively few companies involve their customers in planning and review meetings or in "focus groups" to gather information on the customers' perceptions of their needs and desires. A few companies have set up group meetings with their vendors. One invited the chief executive officers of its many vendors to a strategic planning conference in which the CEO of the prime company reviewed the 1980s and discussed anticipated challenges for the 1990s.

Dan Alspach and Jack Farnan of Orincon Corporation, in a published paper entitled "Strategic Partnering," pointed out that companies and subcontractors far too often pursue their own agendas to the exclusion of the other's best interest. Both entities need to communicate more clearly and more often. They need to talk openly and try to understand problems that are unique to each as well as common. In essence, they need to work as business partners. If each partner better understood the long-range objectives of the other, each would be in a better position to collaborate.

Later in their paper they add: "Mutual trust must be developed. If subcontractors are convinced that the primes are just using them and will discard them at the first opportunity, partnering will be hindered. If primes are concerned about subcontractors' abilities to deliver quality product to spec and on schedule, partnering will be hindered. Communication, understanding, and aligning goals and objectives will all help develop the trust that will be needed."

It is easy—and perhaps typical—for customer-vendor relationships to be seen as win-lose opportunities. In win-lose environments, the adversarial relationships of the parties can jeopardize the integration of multiple group efforts that must function smoothly if the best interests of the ultimate user are to be served.

The concept of just-in-time (JIT) customer-vendor delivery and inventory management demonstrates teamwork processes; the customer and vendor maximize teamwork to minimize in-process inventories for both organizations. Under more traditional systems a vendor will produce goods that are then moved to a warehouse and ultimately removed from the warehouse and shipped to the customer. The customer company then stores the goods in its own warehouse to be used as needed.

With proper communication, coordination, and cooperation, goods produced within a JIT program are shipped directly to the customer and immediately placed at the point of use on the production line. In a dramatic JIT application, metal vendors ship molten metal by special trucks so that the molten material arrives just in time to be poured into molds prepared and waiting in the customer's casting department.

Close customer-vendor coordination may take a number of other forms. One large company invites key members of customers' organizations to join them at many, but not all, of their management retreats. At these retreats, 10 to 20 percent of the participants are customers who can help the vendor organization address such questions as: What is working well for the customers? What isn't working as well as the

customers expected? And what needs and interests are anticipated by the customers in the future?

Many vendor companies have teams that visit customers
for days or weeks at a time to coordinate designs of particular
interest to the customers. In some cases employees from an
organization may work full time in customer or vendor facilities for months or even years, taking up residency in the
community of the organization being visited.

In any relationship, if one party wins and another loses
continually, the relationship will become adversarial and will
ultimately deteriorate. Customer-vendor relations are no different. They should be built on:

- mutual trust and understanding
- agreed-upon expectations
- awareness of the potential benefits to each party
- commitments to make them work
- open feedback regarding feelings
- anticipation of ways to resolve any potential differences

Better communication, coordination, and cooperation
through customer-vendor teamwork? Why not?

Chapter 18

What about the Batboy?

> *A hundred times a day I remind myself that my life depends on the labors of other people, and that I must exert myself to give, just as I have received and am receiving.*
>
> **Albert Einstein**

*T*om Peters points out that the key people who contact your customers to help them buy your products or services, who make the products or render the services, and who interact with customers if something goes wrong tend to be treated with the least respect by others in your firm. They are the clerk in a store, the long-distance operator or telephone installer, the airline ticket agent or cabin attendant, the delivery person, the ticket-taker, the waiter or waitress, the gas station attendant, the salesperson, or the receptionist.

People with titles such as these often are referred to as "just the batboy" or "just the receptionist." They often get little respect, relatively low pay, limited information from above, and limited coaching and guidance regarding the importance of customers, vendors, teamwork, and the need to pursue excellent relationships as well as excellent results. Consequently, they also tend to be limited in opportunities for achievement and recognition. It should be no surprise that deprivation leads to reduced morale, which exemplifies itself via expression of negative attitudes toward associates, customers, and others outside the organization.

In a study made during 1980 and 1981, it was found that where you find good customer relations, you find accompanying good employee-management relations. Conversely, in the absence of a positive internal atmosphere, there will be less-than-admirable customer relations.

How many self-made dynamic entrepreneurs have short memories of the days when they were "just a . . . ." How soon is forgotten what it was like to "pay their dues" or "learn the ropes" in the operating-level ranks. Diminished in their memories, too, are the frustrations they experienced when managers disregarded their suggestions. Some may have even been put down by being told to mind their own business and just do what they were told! Surely, remembrance of such times early in their careers would strengthen interest in and respect of the organizationally junior people now working for them.

Similarly, the dynamic MBA may look with disdain on a less-schooled counterpart. People with a lot of degrees sometimes fail to recognize that *schooling* is not the same as *education,* nor is it necessarily preferable to experience, skill, insight, creativity, wisdom, sensitivity, and understanding. However credentialed a person may feel, the importance of mutual consideration and respect must not be underestimated.

In all organizations, people on the firing line have a plethora of contributions waiting to be offered. In many companies these natural resources lie dormant. These employees are quick to learn, sometimes through painful lessons, that they were hired "to do or die, but not to question why."

Perhaps one of our greatest opportunities in this country is for supervisors at all levels to listen more —truly listen—to the people reporting to them. The concept of asking facilitative questions and listening as a highly effective approach for team leaders is the basic message of one of my prior books, *Lead, Follow or Get Out of the Way.* My advocacy is not for the democratization of management responsibilities nor for majority rule as a basis for decision making. It is simply for the very rational pursuit of participative leadership (employee involvement and empowerment) so that there will be additional information available to decision-makers and greater commitment on the part of those who will be carrying out the decisions once they have been made.

As noted earlier, Galileo said, "I never met a person so ignorant I couldn't learn from him." He didn't add, ". . . except for the people who are just clerks, operators, or at the bottom of an organization chart." If Galileo could learn from everyone he met, isn't it likely the rest of us could too?

In the early 1940s our network of federal interstate highways was being established, and a hapless trucker learned the hard way that one of the overpasses had insufficient clearance for his truck. He could not move forward. He could not move backward. And for hours he and dozens of onlookers pondered the predicament. Finally, a five-year-old girl tugged on her father's arm and inquired, "Daddy, why don't they just let the air out of the tires?" They did, and this true story became a delightful classic portraying the wisdom of those whose opinions, for one reason or another, we often may tend to discount or disregard.

So how about the batboy? Let's include him on the team!

One of our most fundamental individual needs is for a good self-image. Those who lack a good self-image often will tend to be insecure and defensive, and they will develop behavior patterns inconsistent with fully effective teamwork relationships. Without self-respect there can be little or no mutual respect. Defensive barriers will inhibit the building of trust bonding and optimal teamwork.

William James observed, "The deepest principle in human behavior is the craving to be appreciated." If we think of those working for us as "just a . . . ," we are very likely to be sending out signals that we do not hold them in high regard. It is also probable that with such thoughts, we will not seek out subordinates' ideas to contribute to potentially more sound decisions on our part. It therefore will be obvious to subordinates that their opinions, and consequently they themselves, are not held in high esteem—even if we proclaim otherwise to them periodically. Our positive comments will lack credibility since, as Ralph Waldo Emerson has said, "What you do speaks so loudly I can't hear what you are saying."

The leader who listens effectively to subordinates, and encourages expanding effectiveness and efficiency boundaries, will reap benefits in several ways. He or she can:

1. Gain additional information upon which to base decisions. Workers can recommend major improvements that might be made, but they learn to volunteer their ideas only when there is a receptive atmosphere.
2. Give subordinates a greater sense of achievement. Participation in the delineation of goals and strategies breeds a sense of involvement that yields a sense of achievement and high morale.
3. Provide a sense of ownership to the executors. An employee is likely to feel involved and committed if input has been considered before the decision is made, even if the decision is counter to the employee's input—particularly if the supervisor subsequently goes the extra step of explaining *why* the decision has been made.
4. Improve the organization's results. The successful achievement of the organization's goals is the ultimate purpose for group activity. It will follow as a consequence of the benefits described in items one through three above.

The challenge of developing an inspired group of subordinate teammates is facilitated to the extent the group is successful in recruiting and selecting outstanding people. Subordinates who are bright, analytic, creative, innovative, and dedicated will be more concerned than others about being heard and involved. They not only will be more easily frustrated if their opinions aren't heard, but also will be more marketable to other organizations than those with less ability. As a result, in an intellectually sterile atmosphere where subordinates' opinions are not solicited as an inherent part of the decision-making process, the best people get most frustrated most quickly—and leave—while the others who remain in the nonparticipative atmosphere have little chance to grow.

Some supervisors appear to operate with the assumption that they are expected to know so much that they shouldn't have to ask for others' opinions, or that it would be a sign of weakness to do so. This perception of the role and appropriate posture of a leader is terribly unfortunate! Supervisors should heed the old adage that nobody is perfect. Not even those in supervisory roles are expected to be perfect. And those who try to fake levels of wisdom beyond their actual imperfect abilities will, in fact, be seen as pretenders who carry an unnecessary burden of low credibility.

When managers discuss their reluctance to seek the input of subordinates, one often can sense that feelings of insecurity may be an underlying cause. By handling decisions alone, insecure managers may be comforted by behaving as if they are good enough to steer the group's course without help from others. It is far more likely, however, that managers who do not practice the participative involvement of their subordinates fail to do so for either or both of two other reasons.

First, the manager may not realize how important it is for team members to feel good about themselves and to feel appreciated by others. It simply may never have been brought to the manager's attention, or understood, or accepted as a high priority worthy of active pursuit.

Second, and likely to be related to the first point, is the age-old cop-out that "I don't have time!" The fact is, we all have twenty-four hours a day, and we allocate our time according to our priorities. If a manager is wise enough to be concerned about associates' attitudes, he or she will find the time to help them enhance their sense of self-worth. In so doing, he or she will quickly see the positive impact from the investment of just a few minutes per day to improve relationships while driving toward results—with the batboys as well as the superstars.

Chapter 19

Using Commando Tactics With Special Teams

We must indeed all hang together, or, most assuredly, we shall all hang separately.

Ben Franklin

*O*rganizations, like people, develop habits in the way they handle "business as usual." At best, these habits are rhythmic, and work flows smoothly, effectively, and expeditiously. However, habits can become traditions that eventually hamper an organization's ability to respond quickly and flexibly to new challenges. New challenges, emergencies, or crises also may be particularly complex, requiring special dedication on the part of a few key people with exceptionally high skill levels. Although the general functional specialists may do quite well on the not-too-demanding jobs undertaken during periods of traditional business activity, on occasion rallying a particularly talented group from various disciplines may be justified.

In maintaining law and order, a police force will provide continuous coverage through multiple shifts. Routine surveillance, patrol, and administrative efforts are geared to protect the citizenry. But when months of routine detective work culminate in a major drug bust, the services of a Special

Weapons and Tactics (SWAT) team may be needed. Similarly, military organizations may call on commando teams to achieve specific missions which are perhaps limited in scope, but of critical importance.

Business, civic, or other organizations also establish special teams to handle particularly complex or urgent matters. They may be called task forces, temporary committees, commissions, blue-ribbon panels, or even grand juries. Project teams may also be established by enlisting representatives of various specialized groups or factions as members. An engineer, a marketer, a financial analyst, and a manufacturing representative might be set up as a team to develop a new product or solve a particularly challenging problem. In a high-tech or R&D organization, the project team might consist of specialists knowledgeable in signal processing, artificial intelligence, operations research, etc. Such a team will operate with substantial latitude and authority, permitting it to work expeditiously without having to conform to the organization's normal procedures and approval cycles.

In a traditional organization that is functionally organized, there may be departments for research, engineering, marketing, administration, organization development, etc. Within the technical departments might be groups specializing in various engineering and scientific disciplines. Specialists within each department work side-by-side with others having similar skills. They have the benefit of camaraderie with people in their own field with comparable interests. They have the potential for mutual assistance in addressing issues within the scope of their specialty. They also can help each other learn and grow, if only just with regard to skills within the common specialty.

The manager in charge of a functional department such as engineering (or a sub-group such as ocean sciences) must decide, presumably with help from peer managers, what the priorities should be for the department and its members. Should all the engineers in the department work on a particular project until its design has been completed, and then turn to other design or redesign projects sequentially? Typically, the engineering manager will assign engineers to each project, matching their skills and number to the nature, size, and priority of that project.

Functional structures facilitate interactions of engineers with engineers, accountants with accountants, and so forth. However, they may leave each project without a designated coordinator or leader to be responsible for that particular project's success. The expeditious pursuit of project completions therefore may be subordinated to the pursuit of goals of more interest to the groups of functional specialists. For example, the manufacturing manager and his or her subordinates may focus more attention on reducing the direct labor costs from 18% to 17% than on the maximizing of customer service and the long-term success of a particular product, product line, or project. Or a group of specialists might get so enthralled with pioneering work in their field that they lose sight of the need to meet the deadline delineated in the contract.

People with similar professional skills feel relatively comfortable when gathered with their own kind. It is not surprising that groups of specialists find it relatively easy to communicate, coordinate, and cooperate with people of similar skill within their own functional groups. The challenges of communication, coordination, and cooperation become somewhat more complicated when interdisciplinary interactions are required, and frequently contribute to the interdepartmental "we-they" syndrome discussed in earlier chapters.

Some organizations structure themselves on the basis of project groups. Instead of managers heading various functional departments, each manager heads one or more projects. A project manager supervises an eclectic group with substantial autonomy. Managerial focus centers on the satisfactory completion of the project, and not on polishing or aggrandizing a particular functional skill. Each project, therefore, can be viewed as a mini-business. The project manager's role is to oversee the planning and clarification of the project's scope and objectives, the delineation of intermediate and final deadlines, the acquisition of people with talents in the disciplines needed, and the coordination of this array of professionals for the successful fulfillment of the group's project objectives. Each project group has a single purpose, and most of the key decisions for the project are clearly those of the project manager.

With all of its virtues, a project-based organization also has its potential weak points and compromises. Highly independent project managers may duplicate facilities in their dedicated pursuit of project goals. When a project team is formed with various types of specialists, each team member ties perceptions or realities of job security to an understanding of the duration of the special contribution needed during that project's life cycle. A project team member may be anxiously concerned regarding job security or further career potential once the group no longer needs his or her contribution, or when the project is finished. People on project assignments also are likely to feel like hard-pressed practitioners with less opportunity to stay at the cutting edges of their respective specialties than their functionally oriented counterparts. Finally, as projects come and go (or grow and shrink), the organization theoretically will be faced with sporadic but continual campaigns for hiring and laying off talented people. And it won't take many project cycles before desirable people view the company as a low-security employer.

In an attempt to develop an organization that enjoys most of the benefits and minimizes the limitations of both functional and project structures, NASA created a "matrix approach." Numerous organizations subsequently have followed NASA's lead.

The matrix organization uses functional departments to recruit, select, and develop pools of talented specialists. From these company pools, project managers recruit talented people needed to support projects, and specialists return to functional pools when their usefulness on the project expires. While maintaining their project-team membership, specialists may enjoy continuing communication with their functional peers (including some elite functional gurus), and periodically may tap into their advanced (or at least collective) wisdom.

Like all organizational structures, the matrix approach is not perfect. In theory it may seem ideal, but in practice it places specialists under two leaders: the functional manager regarding long-term career issues, and the project manager for short-term project direction. In an ideal world, we could expect ideal communication, coordination, and cooperation. But in our real world, imperfect people find themselves reporting to two imperfect managers and have, at times, described their roles in matrix organizations as perfect only insofar as they are perfectly horrible. Certainly it is fair to say that the matrix approach places a premium on the spirit of cooperation among all functional and project associates.

Since the members of matrix organizations essentially serve two masters (the functional manager and the project manager), a premium is placed on the managers' individual and collective teamwork skills. The functional and project managers must work closely to communicate, coordinate, and review the goals and strategies of the individuals working for them and then collaborate carefully on performance reviews to assure fair appraisals. The success of this system relies on cooperative efforts and positive relationships of all the players. No wonder Peter Drucker and others have advised against matrix structures if there are not compelling reasons to try them.

Nevertheless, the advantages offered by a matrix structure will almost certainly assure its continuance. With their clear, result-oriented charters, special-purpose teams can be charged with clearly defined milestones and results. Because of this goal clarity, the effectiveness of a special team's performance can be evaluated relatively easily. So, counterbalancing the extraordinarily complex relationship challenge is the potential for quick-response flexibility, high levels of effectiveness, and cost-effective levels of efficiency.

The key to success for those who venture down the matrix road will be their ability to provide a culture in which open communication, progressive coordination, and superior cooperation prevail.

Because project teams are like small separate enterprises, the successes and failures of those who lead them will be highly visible. These managers face the risks and enjoy the satisfactions of being in charge of a semi-autonomous venture. Those who do well in project leadership roles become candidates for promotions into more significant managerial roles and perhaps into general management assignments.

Meanwhile, the career paths for functional specialists allow them to move into increasingly significant levels of skill, respect, and compensation. This approach (where highly skilled gurus are recognized and rewarded without moving into management assignments) is called *parallel-path compensation*.

Peak performance teams provide camaraderie, guidance, support and assistance to each other, heeding the old axiom that when all lift, there is no load. And as Walt Disney observed, "There is great comfort and inspiration in the feeling of close human relationships and its bearing on our mutual fortunes—a powerful force to overcome the 'tough breaks' which are certain to come to most individuals and groups from time to time." It is not just the improved spirit or motivation of members of peak performance teams that is important; it is also the resulting levels of effectiveness and efficiency of their coordinated efforts—and that leads us to the next chapter.

Chapter 20

Justifying the Investment In Co-Involvement

The keynote to progress in the twentieth century is teamwork.

Dr. Charles H. Mayo

Why should we take the time to involve others? The most compelling reason is that it works—for a number of reasons!

An organization will achieve results in direct proportion to the knowledge and skills of individuals, coupled with their ability to work together. To make teamwork happen, groups must place communication, coordination, and cooperation high in their value systems and priorities.

How many times have you been involved in crises which (a) could have been avoided or (b) could have been considerably less problematic if the decision-maker had simply asked:

- Who could provide information that might help me (us) make a better decision?
- Who will have to carry out the decision?
- Who will be impacted by it?

And how often have you been left out of a decision-making loop when you could have contributed important information and suggestions?

The supervisor who, as a participative leader, involves subordinates will have more information upon which to base decisions. The subordinates, through involvement, will experience an increased sense of ownership and understanding of the decisions made and will, therefore, execute those decisions more enthusiastically and dependably. Because of their sense of contribution and accomplishment, they will tend to remain in the organization instead of seeking job satisfaction in a more interesting environment. Finally, through continual involvement, the subordinates will learn more about sound decision-making processes, thus continuing to enhance their growth.

A similar situation prevails with peer involvement and interdepartmental teamwork. Any individual or department embarking on a project that ultimately will impact other departments has several potential courses of action. One expedient approach is to pursue the matter without involving other departments until there is a final solution to display for others. The problem is that the would-be hero will be introducing the new development to peer groups who, at best, will be surprised and, at worst, will feel constrained or even attacked by the revelation. Even if the new development is very sound from a technical point of view, the fact remains that the others who must live with it—and make it work—will not necessarily understand it and will have no sense of ownership in it. By plunging ahead unilaterally, the group may complete its development rather quickly, only to face months of agonizing effort to get others to the point of understanding, accepting, and constructively implementing the process or product. During this selling and installing phase, the unilateral developer may alienate the others so badly that the innovation may never get implemented properly.

Such consequences were felt by one electronics company as it plunged into a new performance review effort. A set of review forms was "borrowed" from a neighboring company. Copies were distributed for use by all supervisors in their pending reviews. The whole process was handled expeditiously, and the results were catastrophic.

The supervisors were not familiar with the forms. They were uncomfortable with the approach and awkward in their efforts. Not surprisingly, those receiving reviews were dissatisfied with the results. Discussion among the managers revealed that virtually everyone was rated high; therefore, their own ratings were meaningless. There was, in fact, a small-scale revolt from those reviewed.

The review process needed to be reworked from step one. Representatives of all departments were brought together to discuss what previously had worked well, what hadn't, and what they thought would work well in the future. Every supervisor was able to make recommendations on the approach to be used. The recovery process took several months, and the managers contributed to eight variations of three different forms before locking in on designs they understood and felt could be used successfully. Further, every supervisor was given training and consultative assistance before actually using the revised approach that the group had adopted. Supervisors and subordinates alike agreed that the new reviews were much more valid than the previous ones, and all those reviewed were pleased with the process. Even those whose new reviews were low (including some who were placed on probation) were supportive of the way the reviews were handled! There was not a single complaint.

How logical to involve others who could contribute to enhanced results or who will be significantly impacted by the new development! Yet, how often we plunge expeditiously, taking shortcuts and disregarding the more principled involvement of others. Our motto might well be "Proceed in haste and regret, or regroup, at our leisure!"

When the typical approaches of Japanese managers are compared to those of their American counterparts, two of the key areas in which Japanese methods are considered superior become evident: Their tendency to involve others in pre-decision deliberations, and their style of planning more extensively and for longer-term cycles of results. In both aspects, there is a willingness to invest time and effort at the outset of a deliberation with the intent of reaping dividends subsequently.

In my discussions with thousands of American business people on these matters, *all* have lamented they could be more effective if they planned better in general and were more participative in particular. When asked to explain why they did not pursue better planning and participative approaches, they almost always smiled as they said, "I don't have time!"

Of course, whether anyone has time for any particular thing is strictly a matter of priorities. The supervisor who would like to be either better at planning or more participative (or both) needs only decide to discipline himself or herself to carry through with it!

A team leader transitioning into a more participative style will find that the decision-making process takes longer. In deference to the importance of understanding the compelling reasons for participative decision-making, let's review four key payoffs:

1. The decision-maker can get additional, and often better, information from the others who are involved and who have been observing what has been working or not working.
2. If those who will be involved in carrying out a plan can be involved in the planning and development stage, they will have ownership in the endeavor and greater dedication to its success.
3. The positive rewards of a participative environment will prove more exciting to people who need room to flex their professional muscles, thus permitting the organization to attract and keep people of high caliber.
4. Each person involved in the decision-making process will, through such involvement, have a better chance to learn and grow in professional and managerial expertise.

What a great payoff for those who are willing to seek the counsel of their teammates!

It has been said that the most ridiculous asset is pride and the greatest stumbling block is defensiveness. Don't let either get in your way as a teammate! Let others share in the decision-making process. Review any differences you may have with others and resolve them constructively. You, your team, and our world will be better for it!

Chapter 21

Peak Performance Teams: What Secrets?

Excellence is not an act, but a habit.
Aristotle

I always chuckle when I see titles like "The Ten Secrets of Success". It usually turns out that there are no real secrets to reveal—just an interesting set of basics. Teamwork is no different. There are no secrets—just some interesting basics! So let's review these basics to summarize features we have found in peak performance teams.

Among the successful organizations with which I am familiar, I have found a pattern of basics that have been covered better than usual. These organizations have clear, stretching goals and "can-do" atmospheres. They employ people who have a high sense of urgency, the skill to implement plan-oriented action, and the ability to achieve dependable results.

When we see success, we expect to find an organization that is strong in implementing the following seven points:

1. Team members know and understand their organization's goals, values, and policies. They know where they (and their organization) are going.

2. Everyone recognizes the customer is king. There is a can-do attitude toward fulfilling customer needs, and people are empowered to serve beyond their customers' expectations.

3. Those in charge solicit the ideas of their associates at the very beginning of the decision-making process—including decisions on goal delineation!

4. Team members welcome feedback, solicited or not, favorable or not, from customers and associates.

5. They interact with other associates in ways that reinforce mutual respect as a high-priority element in the value system. They have no associates who are "just a . . . ."

6. They work not just on goals and controls, but also on *process* as well as *content*, and on *principle* instead of *expedience*.

7. Team members serve each other as well as their clients, customers, and constituents as they press toward the achievement of agreed-upon objectives. In short, they empower each other to serve and succeed.

Let's take a look at each of these points in greater detail.

Team Members Know and Understand Their Organization's Goals, Values, and Policies.

If you asked five vice presidents and a president what each understood the goals for their organization to be, there is a high likelihood that you would get six different answers—perhaps not *inconsistent* answers, but *different* answers. And part of their consistency normally would be traceable to vagueness, reflected in such statements as "To grow and be financially healthy" or "To make a profit."

When the answers are diverse among the top executives, there is bound to be even greater uncertainty at lower levels in an organization's hierarchy. Those at the base of the traditional organization pyramid often give answers like, "Who knows?" or "I haven't the foggiest!"

How, you might ask, can people work together as an effective team if they don't have a clear picture of the team's goals? How can they maximize their feelings of achievement if they don't have predetermined goals, the achievement of which is the definition of "success"? The answer to both questions is: They can't!

If we consider effective behavior as behavior that contributes to success, and if success is the achievement of predetermined goals, then each of us can maximize our achievement and the recognition for our achievement only to the extent that we have—and understand—goals to pursue!

In addition to clarifying goals throughout the organization, high-performance companies effectively communicate their basic values and policies. Establishing and clarifying values and policies facilitates planning, setting priorities, and decision making at *all* levels within the organization. Opportunity for everyone for more challenging and fulfilling involvement is facilitated by the goals/values/policies framework.

Optimally performing organizations also are careful to seek a culture in which the goals/values/policies framework is more empowering than restrictive. If care is not exercised, an organization may become paralyzed by a myriad of restrictive regulations aimed at controlling negative behaviors of one or two percent of the employees at the expense of the remainder.

Team superstars predictably are less than appreciative of an environment designed to constrain others. Excelteam members continually revisit, "What is our goal?" and "Are we making progress?" They ask these questions about their long-term strategies, about their tactical efforts, about each meeting they attend, and about such process-oriented matters as their approaches to communication, coordination, and cooperation.

IF YOU DON'T KNOW WHERE YOU'RE GOING,
any path will get you there,
but you won't realize if you're lost,
you won't know what time you'll arrive,
you won't know the dimensions of your challenge,
others won't understand how they could help,
and since you could pass right by without recognizing it,
you won't get the satisfaction of having arrived!

PURPOSEFUL GOALS AND SCORING
IN THE GAME OF LIFE

- Success is the achievement of specific goals.
- Activity without purpose is like archery without targets.
- A sense of accomplishment is the initial reward for the achievement of results.
- Recognition of success enhances the achiever's self-image.
- People with positive self-images can find inspiration to reach even higher.
- Mutual and overall success is the objective of results-oriented teamwork.
- The opportunity to achieve is a powerful motivator and a key dimension in positive work environments.

Everyone Recognizes the Customer Is King

Many great retailers make their mark by being extraordinarily responsive to customers. They strive to exceed customer expectations as the rule rather than the exception.

But customer desire for superior service and the opportunities associated with exceeding customer expectations are not limited to retailers. There are innumerable examples of nonretail success stories based primarily on progressive customer relations and customer service attitudes.

Sadly, the way many customers are treated would suggest focus is too often on what is convenient for the company, not the customer. Surely you have a personal set of horror stories about utility companies and repair services that force you to stay home all day because they won't schedule within shorter intervals. And how about the ones who don't even call to let you know they won't be able to make it after you've waited all day?

I've quit buying at a retail chain that built its reputation on selling quality merchandise at reasonable prices. Years ago they had ample and competent help. But as the years have gone by, the environment in this chain's stores has changed. As their management has focused more on cutting costs, the low priority given customer service has become sadly clear. Paying for merchandise involves lines at the cashier islands followed by a protracted wait so that the cashier can enter not just the price but an incredible array of inventory control information as well. The scarcity of cashiers and the practice of doing the inventory control function while the customer waits may reduce costs, but it also reduces the number of people willing to put up with such poor service.

Or how about doormen who don't open doors for you, or clerks who don't thank customers who purchase, or engineers who want to sell you their components to meet their specifications but not your needs, or suppliers who miss the delivery dates to which they've committed?

Look around you. Mediocrity abounds! And almost limitless opportunities await those who commit—and then follow through—to serve a little faster, a little more dependably and a little more pleasantly.

Organizations that perform well over the long term follow two basic rules:

- RULE I: The customer is always right.
- RULE II: When the customer is wrong, refer to rule number one.

It's amazing how much customer neglect and abuse occurs in so many companies. With the customer service norm fraught with indifference, opportunities abound for excelteams to distinguish themselves in the eyes of their customers. And, as we look at the impact of good or poor customer service (as represented in the following bar chart), we see the benefits of outstanding customer service rendered by high-performance teams.

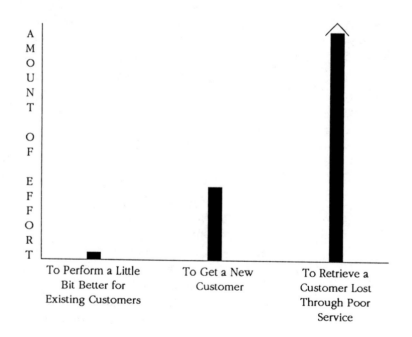

Those in Charge Solicit the Ideas of Their Associates at the Very Beginning of the Decision-Making Process—Including Decisions on Goal Delineation

We already have noted the logic of asking the three key questions:

- Who could provide information that might help me (us) make a better decision?
- Who will have to carry out the decision?
- Who will be impacted by the decision?

Remember, seeking others' input is a strength. Those who are truly strong can build increased respect by not having to pretend they know everything. And for those whose opinions are sought, there is no greater compliment or way to be shown respect.

We know from extensive motivational research that people like to know what is going on around them. They also thrive on having at least some sense of control over their own destinies. Those who are invited to participate in decision-making processes are much more positive about their work environments. Final decisions are not necessarily consistent with every recommendation made. But people need simply to understand that their thoughts, ideas, or suggestions have been solicited sincerely and considered fairly.

Delay in seeking the answers to the three aforementioned questions risks loss in imparting a sense of ownership within the team. The risk, of course, is that this inevitably will reduce the objectivity and flexibility with which other ideas are viewed.

Team Members Welcome Feedback

Most organizations go to great lengths to provide feedback from supervisors to subordinates through periodic performance reviews. Nevertheless, we find that most supervisors in most companies are uncomfortable with their required performance review conversations. Discomfort is compounded by a lack of training and an absence of good role models and coaching. Further, most subordinates feel the feedback they receive is infrequent, insufficient, inaccurate, and perhaps even unfair. Effective teams focus diligently on interactions that enhance these supervisor-subordinate coaching challenges.

"Upside-down" and "lateral" feedback systems are used more frequently in peak-performance organizations than elsewhere. One of the best managed and fastest growing companies we know provides "upside-down" and "lateral" feedback to supervisors through confidentially compiled data gathered from associates and subordinates.

In another company, twenty-one executives engaged in providing mutual feedback. During the process, the facilitator noted that three of these executives were rated significantly more effective than the others in their overall performance. In the detailed feedback, the same three consistently performed in two ways the other eighteen did not. First, all three provided more frequent (twice or four times per year) performance reviews of their subordinates. None of the others conducted reviews beyond the annual reviews outlined by company policy. Second, each had sought feedback from their associates and subordinates. Each had arranged for the collection of feedback data through confidentially compiled questionnaires turned in to their secretaries.

Exceptional organizations also provide for feedback from their customers. Some learn how their customers feel about their products or services through focus groups—regional or national customer "sample" groups gathered to discuss what the customers like and don't like about the vendor.

The chief executives of some organizations place customer contacts and customer feedback so high in their priorities that they personally spend significant portions of their time visiting the customers. Sam Walton was famous for doing so as the CEO of Walmart. Jan Carlzon, who expeditiously turned the unprofitable Scandinavian Airlines into a profitable and distinguished airline, attributes much of his success to the abundant feedback he solicited from his associates and the organization's clientele.

It should not be surprising that members of teams that excel seek and are open to feedback. Whatever the teams' goals may be, the more feedback the members constructively give and receive regarding the progress being made, the more likely the group will perform effectively.

Studies have indicated that of a hundred dissatisfied customers, only four to six will complain. The others, like old soldiers, just fade away. And in spite of the value of feedback, those who complain often are viewed as bothersome malcontents. Excelteams, on the other hand, see complaints and other feedback as providing information that can be used by the team to improve performance and results.

They Interact with Associates in Ways That Will Reinforce Mutual Respect

Those who would lead or play constructive roles in peak-performance teams won't be effective if they talk the talk without walking the walk. They must demonstrate their respect by sincerely seeking others' opinions, being considerate, and pursuing team-building communications.

In short, they add two more rules to the two mentioned earlier in this chapter about the customer always being right.

- RULE III: Always interact respectfully when dealing with everyone.
- RULE IV: When interacting with someone who you think may not deserve to be treated respectfully, refer to rule number three.

They Work Not Just on Goals and Controls, But Also on Process as Well as Content, and Principle Instead of Expedience

When goals and controls prove ineffective, the processes used for installation and implementation likely have been ineffective. And when processes prove ineffective, it usually is the case that expedience replaced principled managerial performance.

The general relationships of goals and controls, process as well as content, and principle versus expedience can be portrayed as follows:

GOALS—CONTROLS
process—CONTENT
principle—EXPEDIENCE

Peak performance teams achieve balanced emphasis:

GOALS—CONTROLS
PROCESS—CONTENT
PRINCIPLE—EXPEDIENCE

Peak performance teams realize that if people have time to react to crises and to fix things that go wrong because they weren't well planned, then there *must* be time to do more planning and be more principled at the outset! The most common excuse we hear for not taking time to plan is "I don't have time." Similarly, those who don't involve their associates appropriately in their decision-making processes and who plunge ahead without consideration and respect for others, invariably hide behind the excuse, "We didn't have time to check with them first."

It has been said that an American manager is considered effective if he or she *responds* well to crises. The effective Japanese manager, by contrast, is described as one who *avoids* crises.

Peak performance teams are principled in allocating time to use good processes. They are sensitive to the long-term desirability of building positive relationships as they drive for results.

Team Members Serve Each Other as Well as Their Clients, Customers, and Constituents

Those on peak performance teams enjoy knowing where the group is headed, what their individual roles are in achieving objectives, how they can do better, and how they are going to be evaluated. They balance the use of their time according to the group's clearly understood goals, priorities, values, and policies.

They also focus attention on building relationships and enhancing teamwork as they drive toward results. They praise and value respectful interaction with others—all others, not just with customers. In fact, many peak-performance teams refer to peer teams as internal clients or customers. The concept that they value serving each other internally as customers and suppliers allows empowerment of the organization's people to serve and succeed. They seek each other's advice. They listen. They delegate. They are considerate, flexible, and supportive of each other. They remember that "We will never be better as a company than we are to each other" and truly that "*Together Each Achieves More Success!*"

Feedback: The Breakfast of Champions

What is our goal? Are we making progress? Peak-performance teams constantly review these questions, not just with regard to annual budget cycles or performance review cycles, but as a way of life! And not just with regard to progress on task-related projects, but also on relationship-related factors, such as improvement of teamwork!

In our society we have to swim upstream when we try to give and receive feedback. We grow up in a culture that is lacking in constructive feedback. When feedback does occur, it usually is unbalanced, with far too high a portion being negative or demeaning. In a recently published study, it was found that American parents criticize and demean their children thirty times as frequently as they compliment them. When a business improves upon the negative-to-positive feedback ratio from which familial relationships often suffer, the benefits are astounding.

The chapters in this section are offered in the hope that you and yours will be able to provide more and better feedback in both your professional and private lives.

Chapter 22

Our Needs and Challenges For Feedback

The trouble with most of us is that we would rather be ruined by praise than saved by criticism.

Norman Vincent Peale

Peak-performance teams are constantly exchanging feedback on what is going well or not-so-well. Unlike athletic teams, teams in industry and commerce seldom have actual video tapes of their performances, except during occasional developmental workshops. They do, however, have the opportunity whenever they wish to stop working on their tasks and devote time to questions about how they have been doing. Most often these discussions are task- and results-("bottom-line") oriented. But to be fully effective, they must provide much more attention to process matters as well.

Peak performance teams explore what elements of their endeavors are effective. Teammates attend to the group's goals and provide feedback to ensure they are clear and consistent in the minds of all involved. What are the group's values, policies, and priorities? What approaches or procedures have been working well? What approaches are being used less effectively? What ideas exist for improvement? In all these discussions, attention should be focused not just on things, but on people—their communications, understandings, feelings, attitudes, coordination, and cooperation.

Let's observe a dental office. One day, the dentist snapped at his assistant because something was not exactly as he wanted it. The assistant was irritated by the criticism—more because of the unpleasant manner of delivery than whether or not there was some justification for the dentist's concern. The assistant said nothing to the dentist. But later the assistant complained to an associate that the dentist had snapped at her, and they commiserated about how unfortunate they were to work in the environment.

By the way the situation was handled, one opportunity was lost and a new challenge was born. First, because the dentist was not made aware of how the assistant felt about his public criticism, he lost an opportunity to improve his behavior in similar situations. Second, in sharing her negative feelings with another worker, the criticized assistant fostered internal strife. And you can bet negative attitudes within the office would be transmitted to the patients one way or another.

How much better it would have been for the assistant and the dentist to have a calm post-incident discussion. They could have discussed the following questions:

- Exactly what went wrong initially that upset the dentist?
- How can all involved reduce the probability of similar future occurrences?
- In the event the dentist is again disappointed or displeased by the staff, how could he most constructively address the issue?

Episodes such as described above occur daily, not just in professional offices, but throughout society. However, many people go through their lives finding it very difficult to give, receive, discuss, and benefit from feedback.

It's very easy in the short run to make quick decisions on our own, to be curt and directive in instructions, to be demeaning or even insulting when providing feedback, and to be offensively aggressive while winning arguments to the detriment of the relationship. Yet it takes little additional time and effort to encourage others' contributions and feedback on current and pending decisions, to encourage involvement, to ask for commitments instead of demanding them, to be constructive and supportive when seeking improvement, and to be able to disagree without being disagreeable—and thus to capitalize on the creative ideas and support of all those who can contribute to making good things happen.

To improve the way one interacts, he or she must take an appropriate attitude toward others—the willingness, desire, and commitment to provide mutually constructive feedback. Through open communication those involved in group endeavors can help each other improve their individual and collective efforts. They can build their mutual understanding not only of their goals, but also of the ways they could more effectively collaborate in pursuing these goals. Improved understanding of each other's desires and needs, when achieved with the nominal investment of coordinated time and effort in the short run, will yield wonderful long-term results.

Traditional supervisor-to-subordinate feedback approaches have been of limited value and have resulted in considerable frustration, as noted in the outline on the next page.

Feedback—Is It Truly The Breakfast of Champions?

How does an excellent manager know he or she really is excellent, and how can the good manager know if his or her growth is helping him or her move closer to excellence? Through short-term task achievement? Through contributions to the organization's long-term success by more effective and consistent task accomplishment? Through the improving teamwork and relationships among those whose effectiveness and efficiency depend on the quality of their communication, coordination, and cooperation?

Feedback for Performance Improvement—
Some Traditional Challenges

1. Feedback to managers traditionally has come almost exclusively from "the boss," so it has been limited to only one person's perceptions.
2. Feedback discussions normally have had the avowed purpose of serving as the basis for both employee growth and compensation. In practice, parties have tended to focus on the compensation ramifications at the expense of addressing growth aspects.
3. As each manager has pushed toward tasks and results, he or she has tended not to address the processes being used in the constant rush for the results.
4. With heavy time utilization pressures, there has been a tendency to focus on problem correction and to limit discussions and compliments about progress.
5. Most managers have not had a chance to observe good feedback and have not been educated in effective ways to give or receive it.
6. When pay raises or promotions are at stake, those who could benefit in the long run from constructive feedback are likely to opt for shorter-term rewards by not openly admitting shortcomings, and pretending to be more effective than they are.
7. Individuals have not understood, or accepted, the idea that their growth is their own responsibility—not the responsibility of their associates or the company.

And how can progress be recognized and understood? Through a combination of clearly understood goals and objectives and corresponding feedback of both quantitative and qualitative input? How else, if one does not know the target for excellence and success and if one doesn't benefit from information on whether one's actions are contributing to progress?

Is it any wonder that many have come to appreciate the fact that feedback is the breakfast of champions?

Without evidence of how they are doing, how can any team know how to get better? If they don't know whether they've succeeded or failed, how can they be interested in what they are doing, much less how they could improve?

Most supervisors find it difficult to give, or receive, good constructive feedback. They are often blamed, but they are seldom trained in the process. No wonder we hear the employees' lament: "We the uninformed, working for the inaccessible, are doing the impossible for the ungrateful."

Good leaders and team members learn that to optimize their long-term effectiveness, they must learn to express themselves honestly and appropriately. They:

- discuss impressions rather than make accusations,
- make requests rather than demands,
- offer suggestions rather than complaints, *and*
- issue invitations rather than mandates or ultimatums.

In short, they help each other feast on feedback, the breakfast of champions!

Feedback—Yes, It Is
The Breakfast of Champions

"Know thyself." (Socrates)

"Oh wad some power the giftie gie us,
To see ourselves as others see us." (Robert Burns)

"Three men went down the road, as down the road went he,
The man he is, the man they saw—
And the man he wanted to be." (Unknown)

"The fault, dear Brutus, is not in our stars, but in
ourselves." (Shakespeare)

"The greatest weakness is the awareness of none." (Unknown)

"He who knows others is learned.
He who knows himself is wise." (Lao Tse)

"To be truly strong, know your weaknesses." (German proverb)

"He who would defend his weaknesses can keep them—and
probably will!" (Unknown)

"To err is human; to not learn from it is stupid." (Lundy)

"Seek out people who don't hold you in awe, who are willing
to challenge you, even if they're wrong." (Richard P. Feynman,
Nobel Prize-winning physicist)

"In the case of any person whose judgment is really deserving
of confidence, how has it become so? Because he kept his mind
open to criticism of his opinions and conduct." (John Stuart Mill)

Chapter 23

How to Give and Receive Feedback Effectively

Honest criticism is hard to take—particularly from a relative, a friend, an acquaintance, or a stranger.

Unknown

Various research studies have shown that achievement and recognition for achievement are keys to high levels of motivation over long periods. A.H. Maslow and others have written extensively about our hierarchy of needs. Our basic needs for survival include air, water, food, and shelter. After these basic needs are addressed, what really turns us on— what helps us perform at extraordinary levels—is the combination of achievement and recognition for achievement.

People who feel good about themselves tend to perform well. Those with a good self-image need not be defensive. They can focus on achieving new goals at higher levels of performance. They are more likely to be pleasant, interested, flexible, cooperative, and supportive of others. Furthermore, research has shown that the way employees treat customers is directly related to the feelings of the employees toward their management and corporate culture. Good feelings about the company lead to good attitudes toward customers.

If we deal with others respectfully, we can help one another maintain our good self images, and we will tend to welcome opportunities for mutually beneficial interactions. And as we move along the path to our ultimate demise, each of us feels better when we believe that the "RIP" on our gravestone will signify "Really *Important* Person" rather than "Really *Insignificant* Person." As William James said:

No more fiendish punishment could be devised, were such thing physically possible, than that one should be turned loose in society and remain absolutely unnoticed by all the members thereof.

So, if achievement and recognition are so important, it behooves all team members to help each other develop feelings of accomplishment and importance. And if success is defined as the achievement of predetermined goals, then it is imperative that team members clearly understand their goals, how well they are progressing, and how they might progress even better or faster!

Optimal work relationships can't prevail unless those involved in the organization develop and maintain an open, communicative environment where feedback thrives. Mutually respectful relationships can be built and lead to effective team performance if those involved provide feedback to one another in a calm, constructive, sensitive manner.

The Supervisor-Subordinate Conversation Guide

Many managers have found the following "Supervisor-Subordinate Conversation Guide" constructive in coaching situations. It works best when the reviewer and the reviewee each note comments and make copies to exchange with one another at the beginning of their conversation. To convert these questions into a useful form, simply generate a brief heading and list the questions (like the ones that follow) on the front and back of an 8½″ x 11″ page.

1. What do you understand is the nature of your job? What are your general responsibilities?
2. In what respects has your performance always been good?
3. In what respects have you improved recently?
4. In what respects do you think you could improve more?
5. What could/should you do to achieve that improvement?
6. What are you actually doing to achieve that improvement?
7. In what ways could I help you improve?
8. In what ways could others help you improve?
9. What are your aspirations, long-term goals, and plans?
10. What other matters should we discuss regarding your performance, needs, and interests?

Although subordinate coaching tends to be poorly handled, the feedback among peers and departments on how to improve teamwork is worse. What an opportunity there is for people to continually ask each other how they can work together more effectively!

For effective teamwork feedback, people should more often:

- describe and discuss the specific situation
- identify specific behaviors
- discuss the perceived impact on themselves, others, and task results
- discuss potential improvements or solutions

As listed above, to successfully provide feedback, those involved should focus on specific situations and behaviors, defocusing from another's traits or personality. The following are guides for giving effective feedback to teammates.

How to Give Positive Feedback

Your goal in providing positive feedback is to help the recipient realize how his or her behavior is having a positive impact on some person, thing, or group. This feedback will help to enable the recipient to apply more broadly, or enhance, behaviors that are having positive results. Your positive feedback will tend to be most beneficial if you:

1. Comment on specific acts or events. This will help the recipient have a clear understanding of the particular behavior causing positive impact.
2. Reinforce why or how the positive results occurred. This will build understanding by the participant regarding what in the behavior was so beneficial and might be repeated advantageously.
3. Be generous with praise—but always sincere. When people are doing well or getting better, they deserve to be complimented. However, undeserved positive feedback could reinforce wrong behavior. Feedback which lacks credibility will jeopardize any positive relationships that may have existed previously.
4. Give appropriate public credit. Take every appropriate opportunity to credit other contributors when giving oral or written reports on progress.

How to Give Constructive Feedback For Improvement

When giving constructive feedback, your goal should be to help the recipient obtain information about how he or she might alter behaviors. Three key factors will determine the potential benefit of the feedback. First, and most important, is the receptivity of the recipient. Second is the approach of the person providing the feedback. Third is the credibility of the information itself.

1. Be sensitive to the recipient's readiness. Even those who boldly proclaim, "Tell it to me as it is!" may, in fact, not be ready to receive the messages you are ready to deliver—particularly if the information is delivered harshly or is surprising in its content.

2. Use considerate phraseology. You can provide information helpfully with a high probability that it will be useful. If information is presented demeaningly, it is likely to be rejected or to make the recipient defensive. The recipient's self-esteem should be protected.

3. Be clear and specific. Do not beat around the bush in attempting to be considerate. Ambiguity or vagueness will tend to confuse the issue rather than facilitate growth.

4. Focus on behavior, not traits. Feedback on particular behavior or actions can be more specific, more easily understood, and more acceptable to recipients than comments regarding traits. Recipients also can see behavioral changes as more easily pursued than attempted trait changes. Traits may be viewed as semipermanent and too delicate to discuss.

5. Express your feelings, not your judgments. The person giving feedback has feelings about specific recipient behavior, but can only speculate about the motives behind the actions.

6. Be timely. When feedback occurs promptly, the memories of those involved are likely to be much more accurate than after the passage of time. Even current perceptions are likely to differ, and the longer the delay before they are discussed, the less likely the differences will be shared constructively.

7. Be brief. Feedback should be a matter of sharing information. Brevity helps prevent information overload and minimizes the risk of triggering defensiveness.

8. Confirm understanding. Seek assurance that the recipient has received his or her feedback without distortion. Evidence of clear understanding can be obtained by having an open discussion of how the recipient would summa-

rize the feedback, and to some extent, by listening to his or her thoughts about corrective action steps.

9. Ask questions. Introductory phrases such as "Do you suppose . . . ?", "Have you considered . . . ?" and "Would it help if . . . ?" can make it easier for the recipient to consider a suggestion without being defensive.

10. Suggest, don't dictate. "Perhaps you could" is a better introductory phrase than "You must" or "You have got to." The recipient doesn't *have* to do anything.

11. Look forward to opportunity, not backward to blame. The feedback game is a game of helpfulness, not a game for demeaning others. Turn from "You surely did make a mess of this!" toward a more constructive "How can we unscramble this and avoid similar recurrences?" Present alternatives that might be pursued in the future.

12. Undertake periodic damage control checks. Keep the recipient's comfort and receptivity in mind. Periodically ask such questions as "Does this seem to make sense?" and "How do you feel about our discussion so far?"

13. Above all, focus on the recipient's needs. It is important that feedback discussions focus on the recipient's needs. Advice can only be defined as helpful by the *helpee*, not the helper! An overly enthusiastic feedback provider may be focusing on his own needs to feel helpful, rather than the recipient's needs.

How to Receive Feedback

People who provide information on how they feel about the various things that you have done (or are doing) are investing their time and effort to make information available to you. Without their efforts, you would not have the information—so you would not have an opportunity to act on it. Whether you act on the information at all, and the ways you react, are entirely up to you! Whatever you do about your feedback, at least be appreciative!

As was pointed out in a prior chapter, "The greatest weakness is the awareness of none"; and "He who defends his weaknesses can keep them—and probably will!" When others extend themselves to be helpful in providing feedback, the recipient should see it as an opportunity to improve and should handle the information accordingly. Because this approach by recipients is easier to recommend than it is to implement, the following guidelines may be helpful.

1. Keep an open mind. The ability to keep an open mind has a major impact on the amount of information absorbed. It also has a significant impact on the willingness of others to continue to make information available to you.
2. Listen to understand. It is important to clearly understand the point or points being conveyed. Listen carefully to what is being said, think about what the sender means, and confirm your interpretation or understanding with the sender.
3. Do not interrupt. Maximized understanding is achieved by minimized interruptions. If you do interrupt, do so politely and in the interest of clarifying what is being said. Otherwise, make notes for use in seeking clarification later.
4. Control tendencies to react immediately. Your best interests generally will not be served by an immediate reaction, either positively or negatively, to what is being said. The initial mission is to seek clear understanding.
5. Seek further clarification, elaboration, and illustrations. Feel free to ask the sender for more information to enhance the team's or individual's understandings. But be careful not to be defensive or argumentative in the process.
6. Keep reality in perspective. When a sender expresses his or her feelings to you, what is being said is reality to the person saying it. You may feel the sender is being illogical or unreasonable, but remember they are expressing how they feel. That is their reality!

7. Express your appreciation. Whether you agree or disagree with the feedback being provided, you can be appreciative of the sender's efforts. You are, in essence, receiving a gift of information.

8. Discuss suggestions for improvement. Those who have been helpful in providing feedback regarding challenges may be good sources of ideas for potential improvement. You also may want to bounce some of your own ideas off of the senders—either in your initial conversation or in subsequent meetings.

9. Obtain more information. Some feedback may be relevant only to your relationship with a particular sender. For other information, you might want to obtain additional views. You may seek more raw feedback, or you may wish to bounce tentative actions off others before pursuing them.

10. Change your behavior. This is more easily said than done. Even minor shifts from old habits may cause anxiety and discomfort. Nevertheless, you will progress in proportion to your desire, dedication, and persistence.

11. Seek feedback on progress. As initial feedback leads to new action steps, continue to seek feedback on performance against new standards.

Constructive Conversation Catalysts

How do you give or receive feedback? Most importantly, you must do it! Often the most difficult part of giving or receiving feedback is getting started. Certain introductory phrases may help you maintain a positive atmosphere and foster useful feedback. The following list of "Constructive Conversation Catalysts" provides useful introductory phrases to help get appropriate feedback discussions underway.

For Giving Feedback and Suggestions

- "Would you be interested in discussing how . . . ?"
- "May I share a few thoughts (feelings) with you about . . . ?"

- "How do you feel about . . . ?"
- "Would you be interested in the way I feel about . . . ?"
- "Do you have any questions (concerns) about . . . ?"
- "Are you aware that . . . ?"
- "Would you like some input (feedback) about . . . ?"
- "Is this a good time to ask you about . . . ?"
- "Do you have a few minutes to discuss . . . ?"
- "Would you like me to elaborate on . . . ?"
- "Does this information seem . . . ?"
- "Am I making sense about . . . ?"
- "Has anyone else expressed similar thoughts about . . . ?"
- "Do you have any idea why . . . ?"
- "Have you considered . . . ?"
- "Do you think it might help if . . . ?"
- "Would you prefer that I (or that I not) . . . ?"
- "Is it possible that . . . ?"
- "Have I said something that may have caused you to . . . ?"
- "Am I sensing that you feel . . . ?"
- "Would you like to think about what we've been discussing?"

For Receiving Feedback and Suggestions

- "Would you share your observations (feelings) with me about . . . ?"
- "May I get your ideas on . . . ?"
- "Would you mind letting me know how . . . ?"
- "Are you saying that . . . ?"
- "Do I understand that the point is . . . ?"
- "Could you help me understand . . . ?"
- "Is there anything else that . . . ?"
- "Do you think it would help if . . . ?"
- "Do you have any particular suggestions regarding . . . ?"
- "Is it likely that . . . ?"
- "Do you think this may be because I . . . ?"
- "How do you feel about . . . ?"

- "How do you think you (he/she/they) feel about . . . ?"
- "Would I sound defensive if I said (asked) . . . ?"

Syrus said, "Many receive advice—few benefit from it!" And Charles F. Kettering noted, "The world hates change, yet it is the only thing that has brought progress." To move toward improved teamwork, organizations must promote the positive changes which can be brought about by increased feedback. Then they can take William Jennings Bryan's words to heart: "Destiny is not a matter of chance, it is a matter of choice; it is not a thing to be waited for, it is a thing to be achieved."

If improved teamwork is an organization's goal, feedback among the organization's associates will allow them to calibrate the extent of their success.

Chapter 24

Feedback and Coaching For Conflict Resolution

You have to listen to adversaries and keep looking for that point beyond which it's against their interests to keep on disagreeing or fighting.

Cyrus Vance

People *are* different. And because they are, they have different goals, values, priorities, attitudes, outlooks, and perceptions. So it is to be expected that individuals may opt for different approaches to contribute to an organization's progress.

People not only have differences—they also may differ regarding their preferences as to how to reconcile their differences. Among innumerable possible approaches, some representative choices include:

1. Withdraw into one's own world to do one's own thing in one's own dedicated—but narrow—way.
2. Reluctantly discuss differences with the attitude (and self-fulfilling prophecy) that it won't do any good anyway.

3. Nicely but unilaterally suggest to the other person that he or she should change to get into step with you.

4. Seek help from a third party to facilitate or mediate, but with the unexpressed hope that the third party will bring the other person into conformance with you.

5. Openly, objectively, and flexibly discuss how you feel, but with an equal interest in learning more about how the other person feels (and why)—hopefully resulting in improved mutual understanding.

6. If necessary, seek help from a third party with the hope that the facilitator can help the parties involved find resolutions or innovative approaches of a win-win nature.

Let's briefly examine each of these approaches.

1. *Withdraw into one's own world to do one's own thing in one's own dedicated—but narrow—way.* When differences occur, they are unlikely to disappear based on the passage of time unless the situation changes. When people with differences continue to interact without addressing these differences, the relationship is likely to become strained or even hostile. At work or at home, people who wish to resolve their differences should discuss them. And in the discussion process, each should deal respectfully with others using the guidelines provided in previous chapters on how to most appropriately give and receive feedback.

2. *Reluctantly discuss differences with the attitude (and self-fulfilling prophecy) that it won't do any good anyway.* One person involved in a difference of opinion may suggest that both views be discussed objectively, or a third party may see the need and suggest a discussion. However, if either or both of the people having the difference participate reluctantly or remain inflexible instead of being truly dedicated to the search for expanded mutual understanding, successful reconciliation is unlikely.

3. *Nicely but unilaterally suggest to the other person that he or she should change to get into step with you.* When one person pushes hard for the other to change, the recipient of the pressure is likely to react in one of three ways: fight, flight, or submission. If the one being pushed chooses to push back, the relationship can quickly become extremely adversarial. Either initially or after sufficient conflict, the recipient of pressure may choose to leave (flight). In industry, this results in turnover. In a family, it can lead to separation or divorce, abandonment or running away. And although submission may lead to a feeling of resolution by the person doing the pushing, the recipient of the pressure may be quietly but unhappily seething inside—and may be watching eagerly for the forced solution to fail or backfire.

4. *Seek help from a third party to facilitate or mediate, but with the unexpressed hope that the third party will bring the other person into conformance with you.* This approach at least opens the door for a sensitive facilitator to objectively calibrate what is going on and, hopefully, to be able to help the would-be manipulator to reexamine his or her own position and approach. Anyone who finds it difficult to listen to an apparent adversary with sufficient openness to build true understanding might be helped if he or she can interact with an objective (and perhaps less threatening) third party.

5. *Openly, objectively, and flexibly discuss how you feel, but with an equal interest in learning more about how the other person feels (and why)—hopefully resulting in improved mutual understanding.* People skilled in process matters as well as content issues often are able to interact with others in ways that minimize the risk that initial differences will produce a downward relationship spiral. If both potential antagonists are sensitive to others' needs and skilled in addressing differences in respectful ways, serious conflict almost always can be avoided. If only one of the parties is process-sensitive, he or she might be wise to opt for help from a third party.

6. *If necessary, seek help from a third party with the hope that the facilitator can help the parties involved find resolutions or innovative approaches of a win-win nature.* Even process-sensitive professionals and caring family members, relatives, or friends at times can assume postures that make it difficult (but, hopefully, never impossible) to voluntarily move away from their own positions and toward the position of someone else, or to a whole new win-win solution. However, a skilled facilitator may be able to bring the parties toward mutual understanding and agreement through a combination of individual and collective discussions. In such cases, the decision to seek help may be suggested by one of the differing parties, or it may come at the suggestion of a caring third party who has become aware of the possible need for intervention.

A few brief suggestions consistent with the prior chapters on feedback may be particularly appropriate when differences occur. The parties involved should:

1. Ask for an opportunity to discuss the issue with each other.
2. Openly express their own feelings without being judgemental of others.
3. Look forward to opportunity, not backward to blame.
4. Stay focused on the issue and don't attack the person.
5. Search for mutually satisfactory or beneficial alternatives.
6. Deal respectfully with one another at all stages of the interactions.

A business owner contacted our company about two highly valued employees who apparently had developed some irreconcilable differences and whose conflict was impacting not only their performance, but the performance of those around them. The owner described Sue Salesperson as an awesome account executive. He had a proper appreciation of her energy, drive, and pleasant demeanor when she was working with prospects or customers. But—and this is what bothered Helen Helper, who was in charge of the customer support office—Sue just couldn't seem to complete the important information needed on order forms for Helen's department to properly serve the customer.

Helen was described as highly knowledgeable, competent, and a perfectionist. She had become increasingly frustrated by Sue continually dropping incomplete order forms in front of her, and she had reacted by exhibiting negative nonverbal messages to Sue every time their work required them to interact.

In fact, seemingly by unspoken agreement, they had allowed their relationship to decline to the point that their conversations were both infrequent and strained.

Sue Salesperson perceived Helen Helper as lacking concern for total responsiveness in the company's search for total customer satisfaction. Helen perceived Sue as aloof and insensitive to the valuable role played by Helen's department. In fact, Helen thought Sue considered her support group to be just a bunch of flunkies. Both Sue and Helen couldn't have been more wrong, but after months of misperceptions, their relationship was spiraling downward. And as often happens, they found it easy to reinforce their own misperceptions through their biased observations of each other.

The owner, observing their strained relationship, was afraid of losing Sue or Helen if they couldn't interact more constructively. He listened to each of them separately and would try to console them—a process which allowed each to reinforce her own perception. Further, the owner was avoiding the uncomfortable process of getting Sue and Helen together to share—and hopefully reconcile—their differences. Frankly, he was afraid that such a meeting would precipitate overt arguments that might lead to a resignation, or to a need to fire one of them.

Because this situation had been festering far too long, by the time I was called in Sue and Helen had really dug in and begun to take pot-shots at each other. Their conflict had begun to impact their associates as well as themselves. The challenge had grown more significant than necessary, and it had the earmarks of an unpleasant as well as a challenging consulting assignment.

My first step was to interview the owner and gain as much background information as I could. I then met privately with Sue Salesperson. She poured forth as I listened, and gradually, with clear but considerate questions, I was able to get Sue to consider that she might get better customer support from Helen's department if she provided them with the complete information needed the first time. We also talked about the fact that Sue probably could save time by not having to call customers to obtain information that should have been gathered in the first place. And, finally, we talked about how Helen might feel "dumped on" because of Sue's style of dropping orders on Helen's desk.

Then came the private conversation with Helen Helper. I assured her she was perceived as performing in a dedicated fashion, and others probably should give her more credit and many more strokes than she had been receiving. And, yes, it must be aggravating to have Sue expect her to drop the phone or anything else when she approached Helen with a question or some more work for her to do. And yes, I could understand how it wasn't much fun working here these days.

In both private conversations I tried to reinforce the person I was talking with—but the reinforcement was for the person, not the position she was taking. While meticulously trying to avoid any perception of favoritism, I pursued three objectives in these private sessions. First, I tried to help each to develop a more empathetic posture relative to the other person. Second, I tried to help each of them examine their own actions and reactions more introspectively. Third, I prepared both Sue and Helen for a joint meeting with me—a step which the owner had accurately predicted would not be high on either Sue's or Helen's list of positive anticipations.

At the outset of our joint meeting I spoke briefly not only about their perceptions, interests, and needs, but also about those of the owner. There was then a brief period of mild self-justification and dart throwing by each of the participants. But we quickly set up some plans so they could look forward to opportunity rather than backward to blame. They also agreed that it would be helpful to minimize mutual interruptions by sitting down together late each morning and late each afternoon for ten to fifteen minutes to calmly and professionally review all new orders and other matters of mutual interest.

The final step in my strategy was to meet with Sue, Helen, and the owner to discuss our progress and how the three of them could reinforce their potential future success. Because the owner remained uncomfortable about this sort of meeting, it wasn't held—much to my concern. Nevertheless, the latest report from the owner is that Sue and Helen have been working together just fine for many months. No, they are not the best of friends, nor were they expected to be. But they *are* teammates.

When differences between associates, family members, friends, or even countries are causing either or both to develop negative feelings, they have little chance of progressive and peaceful resolution unless the parties will discuss the issues open-mindedly. And since the longer chasms exist, the deeper they are likely to get, those interested in working together constructively should address their differences sooner rather than later.

Teamwork for Spectators and Others

What is this section doing in a book on how to achieve peak performance teams in business? If these thoughts haven't occurred to you yet, they might as you read this section.

There are a number of reasons why this section not only has been included, but also why I feel it is important.

First, this book's potential contribution was never intended to be limited just to teams performing in industry and commerce. Indeed, some of my most gratifying retreats have been those I facilitated for university, religious, law enforcement, government, and volunteer groups.

Second, understanding and learning often can be enhanced when reviews include new views. So, to help assure or reinforce in-depth understanding of the generic principles of teamwork and empowering leadership, this section offers additional insights by looking at the communication, coordination, and cooperation challenges and opportunities within families and society.

Third, a number of executives who were asked to "beta test" this manuscript in its semifinal form responded with comments such as:

"I particularly enjoyed the chapters on teamwork in the family and community. It's important to see the relationship between one's role as an employee and that of a family member or citizen."

We have heard innumerable managers comment on how much more effective they pereive themselves to be as members of professional teams as contrasted with their perceived performance as members of their family or society. It was no surprise, therefore, when a reviewer said, "I found Chapter 25 to be personally valuable."

Most people seem to identify the word "organizations" with companies. They think of the collection of people involved in running a high-tech research company. Or a factory. Or a store. Or a service company. Or an institution such as a hospital. Or some other profit-making (or profit-attempting) group. Other people might include government organizations, both civilian and military. A few people may even include in their initial vision of "organizations" groups of people in such institutions as schools, churches, synagogues, service clubs, or charities.

Families, too, can be viewed as a type of organization. They have power structures. And they have (or presumably have) peer relationships between spouses and between siblings.

On larger scales, we also can view neighborhoods, cities, counties, states, countries, and planet earth as groups, or organizations (loose as they may be) of constituents or citizens.

People are people, groups are groups, leadership is leadership, and teamwork is teamwork. Yes, within families and also in society as a whole.

So far we've discussed improved teamwork in other types of organizations. In this section we take an overview of the teamwork and leadership challenges within families and society.

Chapter 25

Teamwork in the Family

*The family is the nucleus of
civilization.*

Ariel and Will Durant

In one of our workshops we gather feedback from participants' coworkers to get an understanding of how each participant is perceived by others and to evaluate how coworker suggestions can best be utilized to make the participant more effective. It is astonishing how frequently participants say, as they read feedback from their subordinates, "That's exactly what my kids complain about!" *Too controlling. Doesn't listen. Impatient. Loses temper before understanding situation. Expects perfection but gives no guidance.*

And often they hear echos of their spouse's concerns in the feedback from peers. *Not a team player. Doesn't trust abilities of others. Doesn't listen. Always has to have final say."*

As issues with peers and subordinates are addressed and viable solutions are developed, particpants come to understand how similar action plans can be undertaken for improved family life. *I will listen with an open mind. I will consider others' opinions before taking action. I will treat everyone with respect and consideration.*

During a feedback session with one dynamic executive, I was discussing perceptions of his associates. We talked about the strengths and needs of the organization, and on many of the points his own abilities and style were seen as key factors. Yes, he was admired for his vision, brilliance, and decisiveness—but he also was perceived as allowing little room for his associates to share in the intellectual excitement of the company's endeavors. With a previously underutilized level of awareness and sensitivity, he started thinking about the parallel pattern or authoritarian decision making which charactrized his role as a husband and father, not just his role as a professional. Whereas he previously had had some concern for how things were going at home, he was excited about now having an increased awareness of ways to contribute to improvement.

In an earlier book on leadership, I suggested an analogy between parental authority over children and supervisory authority over subordinates. When power is flaunted, the three classic potential responses will be fight, flight, or submission.

When someone flaunts power or pushes others, the initial instinct is to push back, or essentially to defend one's ground. Either after an unpleasant conflict ensues, or as an immediate response in order to avoid a fight, the person being pushed may back away and leave.

In companies the flight response leads to personnel turnover. With spouses it may take the form of separation and, ultimately, divorce. Flight may occur physically, in which case we call it running away. Or, flight from reality may be pursued through substance abuse.

In the case of submission, the person being pushed may consciously or unconsciously be trying to avoid fighting or leaving. When submission occurs, the junior figure simply follows orders, including, in extreme cases, doing any ridiculous thing he or she may be told to do by the authority figure.

Parents who flaunt their power don't leave much room for their children to see themselves as respected members of the would-be family team.

One way for us to calibrate family teamwork would be to revisit the key points of Chapter 21, "Peak Performance Teams: What Secrets?" The points have been rephrased to correspond with the terms we associate with families as contrasted with commercial, civic, or other groups.

1. *The family members know and understand their family's values and rules. They know where they and their family are headed.*

   What are *your* family's values? Would each member of your family give highly consistent answers to that question? How many would respond "Who knows?" or "You've got me!" or "I assume . . ." or whatever?

   Children's values are most frequently derived from the expressed and demonstrated values of their parents. Remember, actions speak louder than words. Those actions should be reasoned, reasonable, and supportive, not based on solely emotional responses.

2. *Each family member deals with each of the others considerately. There is a can-do attitude toward fulfilling others' needs, and to do so selflessly and beyond the others' expectations.*

   How wonderful it is when one sibling helps another in need. And how heart-warming it can be when a spouse helps perform a function or task that is normally undertaken by his or her mate.

   Parents who place a high priority on helping their children learn will take the time to include them in achievement-oriented activities. Sure, the "help" received from a child may actually increase the time needed to accomplish a task. But if the parent has clearly delineated mentoring as a high-priority role, the task (such as making a bed) becomes not just an end in itself, but also the basis for a learning opportunity.

   An alternative parental approach is to help children develop an understanding of individual responsibilities.

They can also learn, as Winston Churchill said, "Success is never final, and failure is never fatal. It's courage that counts."

A child whose parents have undertaken the nurturing effort required to help in the development of self-esteem and a set of values is much better prepared to resist temptations and to avoid inappropriate behavior in order to gain attention or recognition.

There are many who dedicate themselves to hard work and long hours in their desire to foster success for their families, but who calibrate themselves based on effort expended rather on the results achieved. Certainly you know people who work excessively long hours and justify it as an investment for the family's future financial security. But how well are the needs of a family served by a breadwinner who achieves steady growth in income and net worth, but who is so busy professionally that there is little or no quality time available to his or her spouse and children, the members of his family team? Have you ever known a professional or manager who, close to death, said, "Gee, I surely do wish I'd spent more time at the office."

How about yourself? Do you suppose your spouse or children wish you would have more quality time with them—even if it were at the expense of less money for them (and the family) to spend? Are you one of the innumerable executives who have so much, but who seem to need more, and more, and more? And, in the pursuit of the ever-elusive "more," have you ever counted your blessings and asked yourself how you might better serve your loved ones?

3. *Those in charge solicit the ideas of the rest of the family at the very beginning of the decision-making process.*

Parents too often underestimate the abilities and awareness of their children. Children want to achieve and revel in recognition just as we all do. They will feel more respected and more important if asked for their input.

And if they are included in the intellectual goal-delineation process, they will understand the challenges better, be better prepared to address them, and be more inspired to achieve them.

When a parent barks an order to a child, that child will feel "pushed," just as a subordinate who is barked at by a supervisor does. How much more pleasant, inspiring, and constructive it can be for a parent/child discussion on the desirability of a neat room than to have the parent constantly barking, "Make your bed!"

Could the Chapter 20 questions apply to the way you interact with your family members?

- Who could provide information that might help me (us) make a better decision?
- Who will have to carry out the decision?
- Who will be impacted by the decision?

How will your child's career path and choice of schools be determined—unilaterally by a parent, or following considerable and considerate discussion with your child? Who makes the decisions regarding your family recreation and togetherness, and who else has a chance for predecision input?

Is your family a winning team? Do all members support and encourage each other's efforts and achievements, large and small? Do you all uphold and reinforce the values of your team? Can you celebrate your team's success, or is it time for a team meeting?

4. *They welcome feedback, solicited or not, favorable or not, from each other.*

Many parents have a long way to go in fostering environments characterized by open and constructive give and take. Not just with regard to their children, but also between themselves. Marriage counselors and therapists point out that lack of understanding or misunderstandings contribute to much of the conflict in families, and to a large portion of separations and divorces.

Feedback in businesses should include compliments as well as constructive advice. Feedback within families should be similarly balanced. Families that want to cultivate feedback can focus on two challenges. First, is each member willing to receive feedback and to make it easy for others to offer it? Are the children so fearful of their parents that they wouldn't dare express themselves openly and honestly as to their likes, dislikes, goals, anxieties, concerns, and dreams? And how calmly do the spouses listen to the thoughts being shared by their mates?

Second, have the family members learned to *give* feedback along the lines recommended in the earlier feedback chapters? Families can learn how to provide feedback in ways that are unlikely to trigger defensiveness or anger on the part of the recipient.

When behavior is inappropriate, or deemed inappropriate by someone involved, it can't be corrected unless the behaving party can be helped to understand how it is affecting or impacting others. And when behavior is seen as beneficial, it should be reinforced by others who can offer compliments.

Open communications enhance the ability of family members to understand each other. And those who understand each other are in a position to be supportive. They will know when additional dialogues are needed regarding goals, values, guidelines, and responsibilities. And they will know when and how to more effectively coach and console. They will be able to build on their mutual interests while accepting their differences. And they will know how to provide mutual support, and when to retreat to allow room for individuality.

In short, couples and families who build understanding enhance their chances for positive family relationships. As mentioned earlier, open discussions with mutual respect may not lead either party to change position. The parties can, however, contribute to mutual understanding and thus the acceptance of different opinions without conflict. Harmony, trust, and mutual support do not require forfeiting individuality. Thank goodness! What a dull world it would be if enhancing teamwork required eliminating individuality.

5. *They interact with each other in ways that will reinforce mutual respect as a high-priority item in their value system.*

Many parents underestimate the competence and learning potential of their children (just as supervisors often underestimate the abilities and potential of their subordinates). And when they do, they tend to be slow to release responsibilities to their offspring. Overprotected children thus lack sufficient opportunity to learn responsibility and acceptance of the consequences of their actions. Nor do they have the best shot at taking on responsibilities from which they can gain the satisfaction of achievement and enhance their feelings of self-worth.

Each of us must learn to be responsible for our own behavior and, ultimately, our destinies. We can help our children more by allowing them to take on increasing responsibility, (gradual as the process may be) than by expediently doing everything for them.

By helping to create an atmosphere of mutual respect, one family member can help another feel like more than "just a breadwinner" or "just a housewife" or "just a kid." In short, each will help the others feel good about themselves—and the family!

6. *They work not just on a sense of purpose, but on process as well as content, and principle instead of expedience.*

Achievement and recognition for that achievement are important contributors to a positive sense of self-worth, and family members can enhance their attitudes and morale if they have a sense of purpose.

Parents can help children learn how to maintain a sense of purpose, to understand the realities of risk and challenge, and to enjoy the satisfaction of progress and success. The nurturing parent can ask children about goals and progress, even in such simple ways as asking, "How would you like to learn to tie your shoes?" They can help children clarify annual goals, such as year-end grade point averages. And they can help them learn to use interim checkpoints, such as grade targets during a particular grading period, to increase the probability of success on the longer-term goals.

By supportively asking questions, a parent can help to focus on future opportunities. What strategies do you have to reinforce your recent successes? How do you plan to prevent or minimize future shortfalls? How can I help?

Successful practitioners using goals and controls as a way of life know the benefit of clearly delineated action steps to enhance the performance of team members. One study indicated that American high school seniors spend more time watching television each night than they spend *all week* on homework. If a family wishes to enhance the quality of its children's education, standards might be negotiated regarding study time.

Spouses and parents should heed some words of caution about goals and controls. In industry, the successful use of goals and controls depends on process sensitivity and principled decision-making. Nurturing parents know that encouragement and guidance can contribute more to future successes than criticism which risks a devastating impact. They also focus on what is good for their children, not themselves. For example, a principled parent will not try to relive his or her athletic or scholarly memories by placing pressures on a would-be star athlete or student.

7. *As they work toward the achievement of agreed-upon objectives and the enhancement of the family's values, they interact with respect and serve each other well. In short, they empower each other to serve and succeed.*

Spouses, parents, and children who wish to help each

other maintain high levels of harmony and success may wish to:

- Discuss goals, dreams, desires, and values frequently
- Clarify expectations in advance
- Talk about challenges openly and supportively
- Focus on issues and behaviors without attacking character
- Discuss potential solutions and help to evaluate choices
- Encourage children to be responsible for their actions
- Support taking initiative, such as a part time job
- Coach and caution against becoming overextended with outside activities
- Watch for opportunities to praise and reinforce
- Be patient and supportive while following up on previously understood expectations

Parents should ask what contributions they can make not just as parents fulfilling the needs of children up until they "leave the nest," but also as the mentors and shapers of those who will build society's future. Truly, parents are in positions to significantly impact the future of our society. By increasing our orientation to teamwork in our personal lives, surely it will be more likely that together in our society each will achieve more success! And that is the subject of the next chapter.

According to a Chinese proverb,

If there be righteousness in the heart,
there will be beauty in the character.
If there be beauty in the character,
there will be harmony in the home.
If there be harmony in the home,
there will be order in the nation.
If there be order in the nation,
there will be peace in the world.

ON MARRIAGE AND PARENTING

A good marriage is like a handshake. There is no upper hand.
Arthur Kent

We have careful thought for the stranger,
And smiles for the sometime guest,
But oft for our own the bitter tone,
Though we love our own the best.
Margaret E. Sangster

To maintain a joyful family requires much from both parents and the children. Each member of the family has to become, in a special way, the servant of the others.
Pope John Paul II

Your child will follow in your footsteps more readily than he or she will follow your advice.
Unknown

The biggest disease today is not leprosy or tuberculosis, but rather the feeling of being unwanted.
Mother Theresa

The frightening part about heredity and environment is that we parents provide both!
Reader's Digest, May 1962

If you are successful in your career and with your investments, but not as a member of your family, what good is what you have?
Craig Estes

There are two lasting gifts we can give our children. One is roots, and the other is wings.
Unknown

Chapter 26

Our Teamwork Opportunities As Citizens

Let everyone sweep in front of his own door, and the whole world will be clean.

Goethe

Are you a considerate, principled citizen? Ask yourself these questions to determine your teamwork index. Score yourself as follows: Never: 1; Seldom: 2; Sometimes: 3; Usually: 4; Always: 5

1. When you make eye contact with a stranger, do you say hello, or at least nod or smile?
2. Do you hold the door for someone right behind you?
3. Do you say thank you if someone holds the door for you?
4. When using public facilities, do you leave the restroom as clean as you found it?
5. Do you park your shopping cart off to the side of the aisle while looking for an item on the shelf?
6. When boarding planes, trains, or buses, and when greeting others who are arriving on planes etc., do you make a conscious effort not to block doorways and aisles?

7. At parties do you step back after getting your beverage or hors d'oeuvres so others can have access to the bar or refreshment table?

8. Are you careful not to drive into an intersection until you are sure you will not be blocking cross traffic, causing gridlock when the light changes?

9. When headed straight, do you avoid stopping in the far right lane to enable others to make right turns while the light is still red?

10. Do you use patience instead of your horn when another driver does something that you think is inconsiderate?

11. Do you avoid cutting into lines at banks, stores, restaurants, and ticket counters?

12. Are you concerned about keeping promises to others, including those to meet or to be ready at a certain time?

13. When you are an established member of a group, do you make it a point to welcome newcomers?

14. Are you careful to place your trash in appropriate receptacles, to avoid littering?

15. Do you make an effort to sort your trash for recycling?

16. When you find a wallet, pet, or other property belonging to someone else, do you extend yourself to return it to the rightful owner?

17. Do you respect the property rights of your employer, not removing equipment or supplies for private use without permission?

18. Are you astute but honest in filing your taxes?

19. Are you astute but honest in filing insurance claims?

20. Do you avoid taking unwarranted advantage of opportunities for government or civic assistance?

21. Do you offer assistance to others who have their arms full of packages, suitcases, or children?

22. Do you vote at every opportunity?

23. Are you formally involved in a neighborhood watch program, or do you behave as if you were?

24. Do you conform to speed limits, traffic signals, and other vehicular laws and regulations?

25. Are you careful to not drive while under the influence of alcohol or drugs?

It is not intended that these questions cover the entire spectrum of social behavior. Instead, your answers should be viewed only as indicative of your general attitude toward responsible behavior.

If your average response is 4.5 or above, you may be destined for sainthood. If it is between 4.0 and 4.5, you are probably considered a great friend and neighbor. If between 3.0 and 4.0, you are not likely to have a large and active fan club, but you're not likely to be seen as a problem, either. If your average score is less than 3.0, others may see you as more of a taker than a giver.

Life will not be as good as it could be for any of us if we don't increase our sense of individual responsibility for team success. One sometimes wonders if there is so much attention being given to our *rights* these days that we are losing our focus on our *responsibilities* as citizens, and as the captains of our own fates.

As we accept individual responsibilities to not contribute to social problems, we must also dedicate ourselves to fostering improvement. Surely we individually and collectively can make substantial improvements in such institutions as our educational and government bodies. Our potential contributions can include helping to assure that those running our public institutions will themselves become more responsible.

Many consider our educational institutions to be individually and collectively in disarray. A National Geographic Society study indicated that in 1990 only one out of every seven Americans can find our country on a world map. Among industrialized nations, the United States has the worst literacy scores, and only one in ten of the country's illiterates is getting help. Three thousand students drop out of our schools each day. And our colleges and universities have been criticized for focusing far too heavily on professional research and publication at the expense of quality teaching. On too many

ON CITIZENSHIP

People of widely divergent views in our country live in peace together because they share certain common aspirations which are more important than their differences. The common responsibility of all Americans is to become effective, helpful participants in a way of life that blends and harmonizes the fiercely competitive demands of the individual and society.
Dwight D. Eisenhower

And so, my fellow Americans, ask not what your country can do for you, ask what you can do for your country.
John F. Kennedy

The well-being of worker and employer, of manufacturer and consumer, of economic and political life are all bound together.
Erwin D. Canham

Do something for somebody every day for which you do not get paid.
Albert Schweitzer

We treat this world of ours as though we had a spare in the trunk.
Al Bernstein

Where apathy is the master, all men are slaves.
Unknown

The only thing necessary for the triumph of evil is for good men to do nothing.
Edmund Burke

No man is worth his salt who is not ready at all times to risk his body, to risk his well-being, to risk his life, in a great cause.
Theodore Roosevelt

The strength of a nation does not lie in forts, nor in navies, nor yet with great standing armies, but in happy and contented citizens, who are ever ready to protect for themselves and to preserve for posterity the blessings which they enjoy.
William Jennings Bryan

---

campuses faculty members believe that extensive time spent in quality counseling is time that can't be spent on increasing their prospects for promotion or tenure through research.

I am also very conscious of the need to re-orient our educational institutions to their "customers" or "clients"—the students. As a college professor, I felt it was quite clear that innovative proposals had to pass three tests—and in the wrong order. The first question regarding any proposal seemed to be: Will it be administratively convenient? Second: Will it be convenient for the faculty? And the third, lowest-priority question seemed to be: Will it provide cost-effective benefits for the students?

Early in 1989 the Educational Testing Service reported how American thirteen-year-olds performed on science and math tests. When compared with their counterparts from Canada, South Korea, Great Britain, Ireland, and Spain, they scored near the bottom in science and last in math. Education Secretary Lauro Cavasos was led to ask, "How many times must this nation be reminded of its educational deficit?"

But there are other ways to make our teachers and school administration more accountable. If you have children in school, how recently have you thought, complimented, or complained about the quality of the school environment? And how long has it been since you attended a PTA meeting, or went to talk to people in the school system about needed improvements or outstanding performances? Have you done all that you feel you could have done, or should have done, to push for improvements? If not, why not?

Similarly, how many people do you know who constantly complain about the functioning of local, state, or national government—yet don't even bother to vote? Each fall, nearly two-thirds of our electorate fails to vote in state and local elections. Somewhat akin to the nonvoters are the occupants of the thirty-three million households that didn't return their recent census forms. Worse yet, it is estimated that for every five dollars owed in federal taxes, one dollar is being evaded—a collective amount, by the way, that would go a long way toward eliminating the federal deficit.

We must do more than just complain about our politicians. We must reach out and be involved in fixing what needs to be fixed, or at least be involved in electing those committed to doing the fixing.

Many (perhaps most) people believe that the best hope for a balanced federal budget is the provision of the presidential line-item veto. Proponents point out that many worthy bills being passed at the federal level carry special interest add-ons that collectively amount to many times the expense of the original item. They also point out that a politician's prime objective is to be re-elected, and one way for a politician to gain endearment is to tack on to national bills pork-barrel items of local interest. A cartoon by S. Kelley in the *San Diego Union* addressed this accountability situation. It depicted a big-mouthed voter in six consecutive frames as follows:

Frame 1: "I'll tell you why the economy's in the dumper . . ."

Frame 2: "It's all those self-serving politicians ignoring the needs of the country . . ."

Frame 3: "Voting only the narrow interests of their constituencies!"

Frame 4: "I hope all the incumbents get bounced in November!"

Frame 5: (No comment. Voter thinking with his mouth closed.)

Frame 6: "Except my congressman . . . he brings home the bacon in our district."

Richard Lamm (former governor of Colorado and head of the University of Denver's Center for Public Policy and Contemporary Issues) wrote about "Our Uncompetitive Society" for *U.S. News and World Report* (April 25, 1988). He pointed out how great our challenges are to improve our society together.

- The U.S. spends almost twelve percent of our gross national product on health care; our auto industry spends about eight times as much on health benefits as do the Japanese counterparts; yet we are far from the healthiest people in the world.
- We are the most violent crime-ridden society among industrialized nations, and no competing country must bear as heavy a burden of crime-related costs.
- We are the world's most litigious society, and we support two-thirds of the world's lawyers. We bear not only heavy legal costs, but also heavy insurance costs associated with the fear of litigation.
- Among modern industrialized societies we have the highest rates of drug addiction, teenage pregnancy, and functional illiteracy.

Lamm further challenges us with the following thoughts:

We have a Congress that believes that the way to trim the deficit is to sell public assets, make cosmetic cuts in entitlements and defense and rely on the tooth fairy to make up the rest. Serious efforts to come to grips with the difficult, emotionally charged issues like health care, welfare reform, crime, illiteracy, drug addiction, teenage pregnancy, racial tensions, excessive litigation, and other factors that make America uncompetitive are almost nonexistent.

Will people never quit pursuing their own self-interests? Probably not. But perhaps individuals can be helped to see how their self-interests, indeed, the self-interests of all of us, may be fostered by each of us making more principled and process-oriented decisions.

Great social challenges continue, not the least of which is teamwork among those of differing ethnic and religious heritage. Our great country has boasted that its borders mark the boundaries of the world's greatest melting pot, but much work remains for us to reach the desired qualitative standards. Many challenges also remain regarding the true implementation of equal opportunities for women to enhance their economic, intellectual, and social well-being. And men, as well as women, should be concerned about progress toward equality.

As we noted earlier, we in America may have come over in different ships, but we're all in the same boat now! There is no reasonable objective this great country can't achieve if we are, indeed, in one boat. We only need to take broader, more long-term, and more empathetic views—welcoming and capitalizing on diversity. Let us also be open in communications to build better understanding. And let us not only be *willing* to change, but to *actively pursue* it as well.

When he was asked how he felt about Western civilization, Mohandas Gandhi replied, "It would be a good idea!"

It would be—wouldn't it!

Chapter 27

The Really Big League— International Relations

We are dependent on one another, every soul of us on earth.

George Bernard Shaw

*O*ne world, one people. Will it ever happen?

According to Don Marquis, "The chief obstacle to the progress of the human race is the human race." As mankind has progressed exponentially in matters of technology, information, and knowledge, few would argue that progress has kept pace in international communication, coordination, and cooperation. We need only note that during the last two centuries there has never been a period devoid of international conflict. In fact, there has been a steady trend upward in the number of locations throughout the world where armed conflict exists, and more than coincidentally, an increase in the world-wide inventory of armaments.

Abe Lincoln observed, "From the first appearance of man upon earth down to very recent times, the words *stranger* and *enemy* were almost synonymous. Even yet, this has not totally disappeared. The man of the highest moral cultivation, in spite of all which abstract principle can do, likes him whom he does know much better than him whom he does not know. To correct the evils, great and small, which spring from want of sympathy and from positive enmity among strangers, as nations or as individuals, is one of the highest functions of civilization."

And, as William J.H. Boetcker anticipates, "What a different world this would be if our 'thinking workers' and 'working thinkers' (be they earners or wage payers) would realize that truth, justice, honesty and loyalty plus confidence, goodwill and harmony, will ever be the only possible stepping stones for a greater and better world. For only with such corner stones will mutually advantageous cooperation be made possible."

But progress toward world peace can't occur without the involvement of the world's citizens. Progress only occurs when courageous people seize their opportunities to change things for the better. The consequences of apathy were noted by the moving admission of Martin Niemoeller: "In Germany they came for the Communists, and I didn't speak up because I wasn't a Communist. Then they came for the Jews, and I didn't speak up because I wasn't a Jew. Then they came for the trade unionists, and I didn't speak up because I wasn't a trade unionist. Then they came for the Catholics, and I didn't speak up because I was a Protestant. Then they came for me, and by that time no one was left to speak up."

On a brighter note, Lech Walesa predicts "There will come a time, which I won't see, when narrow Polish problems have been brushed aside, replaced by harmony and peace over our entire planet, and I expect that our children and our children's children will be able to sing another, more positive song. Until that time, we have work to do."

We have work to do? You bet!

One world, one people? Are *you* helping? *Will* you?

ON INTERNATIONAL PEACE AND PROSPERITY

We were born to unite with our fellow man, and to join in community with the human race.
Cicero

We have always held to the hope, the belief, the conviction that there is a better life, a better world, beyond the horizon.
Franklin D. Roosevelt

World peace is not only possible. It is inevitable.
Bahai Teaching

War doesn't decide who is right—only who is left.
Unknown

You cannot shake hands with a clenched fist.
Golda Meir

We must seek, above all, a world of peace; a world in which peoples dwell together in mutual respect and work together in mutual regard.
John F. Kennedy

Only justice, fairness, consideration, and cooperation can finally lead man to the dawn of eternal peace.
Dwight D. Eisenhower

It is understanding that gives us an ability to have peace. When we understand the other fellow's viewpoint, and he understands ours, then we can sit down and work out our differences.
Harry S. Truman

Own only what you can carry with you; know language, know countries, know people. Let your memory be your travel bag.
Aleksandr Solzhenitsyn

Am I not destroying my enemies when I make friends of them?
Abe Lincoln

The Post-game Show

This section provides a set of guidelines on how to achieve peak performance from excelteams. It also challenges you to step up and be counted as a teammate. You can do something about you! You can only set an example for others!

As Albert Schweitzer said, "Man must cease attributing his problems to others and learn again to exercise his will—his personal responsibility." Personal growth and team development may require much effort and perhaps even more discomfort during periods of rapid transition. But Plato observed that "the beginning is the most important part of the work," and Charles Kettering has added: "The world hates change, yet it is the only thing that has brought progress!"

Chapter 28

Ten Facilitating Perspectives

A habit cannot be thrown out the window. It has to be coaxed down the stairs one step at a time.

Mark Twain

Many managers latch onto basic concepts that will help them understand and undertake beneficial behavior changes. They find it helpful to increase their awareness of these basics through analogies or catchy labels. Just think, for example, of the Blanchard and Johnson concept of the "One-Minute Manager" or the delegation concept of "put the monkey on someone else's back" or Jan Carlzon's "moments of truth" referring to every instance of customer or prospect contact. Currently, American industry seems to be focusing on "Total Quality Management" (TQM) which, as we practice it in our firm, might more broadly be called "Total Customer Satisfaction" (TCS).

This chapter summarizes ten facilitating perspectives that might be useful in assimilating and applying teamwork concepts.

For any would-be improved team player, any one of these perspectives may prove to be the key to successful growth. Or two or more may be useful—or perhaps, even all ten! As you consider them, note in particular those which will be the most helpful to *you* in your future endeavors.

By way of review, let's look again briefly at each of the concepts.

Ten Letters with Three Words

America is scrambling to keep up in international economic and technological races. In many respects and in numerous industries we have lost our position of previously undisputed leadership.

Fortunately, hope is visible on the horizon. Those who head organizations of all types are becoming increasingly aware of the virtues of *empowering* leadership and teamwork.

The empowered leader and teammate provides for the participation and involvement of associates—not just in the doing, but also in the thinking. Those who seek to empower others recognize that people are more inspired to implement and complete those things which they have helped create.

The root of the word empowering is "power." And we can gain more power when our human resources become involved in the delineation of plans, decisions, and strategies regarding matters on which they are expected to contribute.

Within the word power is "we." Clearly, no one is as powerful as all of us together. And clearly, Together Each Achieves More Sucess. *We* marshall our *power* more effectively in environments which are characterized as *empowering!*

Empowering. Power. We. As America comes more in tune with these three words, we will as a country become more successful on economic fronts. Indeed, there are innumerable success stories in which the improvement and achievement of empowered groups have been truly awesome. There must be more!

Nine Letters of the Essence

Underlying any purposeful effort must be an *objective*. What goals (also nine letters) are we pursuing? What is our mission? A clear understanding of our purpose, our underlying values, and our priorities will enable us not only to chart an optimal path, but also to evaluate if we are still on course. Indeed, what questions can be more important to an excelteam than "What is our objective?" and "Are we making progress?"

Eight Letters: Flip-Flop

The conventional practice for organization charting is to place the chief executive officer (or board of directors, if the board is shown) at the top of a pyramid. Or if the chart is of a group, division, or department, the person in charge appears at the top of the pyramid. In practice, the subordinates at each subsequently lower level are viewed as serving the person to whom they report. Thus the president (and/or the board) will establish an annual goal or set of goals. Typically the vice presidents will "buy in," and each will see his or her role as providing some specific contribution to the success of the president in attaining corporate goals. The directors in turn will help the vice presidents succeed, the managers will help the directors, the supervisors will help the managers, and the operating level people will help the supervisors.

In this model, the focus centers on helping the boss succeed. Now consider squeezing the sides of the organization chart so that it is reconfigured into a vertical rectangle, resembling an office building instead of a pyramid. Using this analogy, the head of the organization occupies the penthouse with its beautiful panoramic view. Others at lower levels in the organization occupy offices at correspondingly lower levels in the skyscraper. The supervisors wind up on the ground floor. The operating level people (and the customers they serve) thus are relegated to the bargain basement! Is this really what our customers deserve?

By contrast, those who conceptually and spiritually *flip-flop* their organization charts see the head of the organization supporting his or her direct reports, they in turn support theirs, and so on up the levels of the upside down pyramid. With this model, the customers are always given the penthouse and the focus of everyone is skyward—leading toward stellar customer service and satisfaction.

Seven Words and Two Pairs of Rules

Successful teams often speak of two rules as described in Chapter 21:

- RULE I: The customer is always right.
- RULE II: When the customer is wrong, refer to rule number one.

This perspective serves as a reminder not only of this pair of rules, but also the seven-word suggestion to *always interact respectfully when dealing with everyone.* To carry this out, we can be guided by a parallel set of rules as follows:

- RULE III: Always interact respectfully when dealing with everyone.
- RULE IV: When interacting with anyone who you may feel may not deserve to be dealt with respectfully, refer to rule III.

By dealing respectfully with one another, we enhance our self-images, feel good about our relationships, and press toward consistent long-term results.

Six Words in Three Pairs

As first mentioned in Chapter 21, substantial improvement in the long-term effectiveness of a team can be achieved if we change the typical emphasis on these words from this:

GOALS—CONTROLS
process—CONTENT
principle—EXPEDIENCE

---

to this:

GOALS—CONTROLS
PROCESS—CONTENT
PRINCIPLE—EXPEDIENCE

The most effective executives build teams that can achieve peak performance over the long term. They don't work just on goals and controls. They also invest heavily in principled decisions that contribute to improved processes as they drive toward exemplary results. The way people approach goals and controls is at least as important to success as the goals and controls themselves.

Let's consider one other thought about principled behavior employing good process. Are the stripes on the zebra black or white? Similarly, when highly effective managers who use good processes are asked if goal delineation and planning should be from the top down or the bottom up, they very likely will answer "Yes." We suggest that goal delineation and planning should be an interactive and iterative process, with information and suggestions flowing in all directions during the course of several drafting cycles.

Those who unilaterally dictate goals and plans from above lose the opportunity to gain input from subordinates and prevent the subordinates from enjoying intellectual challenges and stimulation. As a consequence subordinates have less growth stimulation, and all involved have less opportunity to understand what is going on around them.

Five Letters on Symbiotic Relationships

For this framework we can return to the cover of this book. It's as simple as TEAMS—Together Each Achieves More Success. You know it. I know it. We all know it. Our challenge is to do something about it!

Four Words about Style

One of my previous books, *Lead, Follow or Get Out of the Way*, focused primarily on the concept of adopting a leadership style or approach described by the four words *ask questions and listen*. Subtitled "Leadership Strategies of the Thoroughly Modern Manager," that book advocated more participative leadership.

How about you? Do you think you might try—sincerely try—to shift more toward asking questions and listening at work? Maybe also at home?

Three Questions Before Deciding

One of the most significant steps you can take toward better team playing is to ask the three questions presented in prior chapters:

1. Who could provide information that might help me make a better decision?
2. Who will have to carry out the decision?
3. Who will be impacted by the decision?

Consider these questions at the outset to help keep from becoming biased toward a preliminary solution. This in turn will help you be more open and objective in sincerely considering the input obtained.

Two Letters about Balancing Behavior

Remember the teamwork concept of R&R which was discussed in Chapter 7—not the military R&R meaning rest and recreation, but our teamwork R&R meaning Relationships and Results. In essence, we are using this framework to reinforce the concept of *process* (how I do or say something) versus *content* (what I do or say). To maintain or enhance our relationships as we strive for results, we must continually consider the processes we use along the way. The payoff comes from consistently better results achieved by those who do so.

One Word in Summary

One word! Wow! This is an interesting challenge, since there are a lot of key words which carry powerful meanings.

Certainly one of my favorites is the word *understanding*. Just think of all the confusion, turmoil, and conflict, which potentially could be avoided through better understanding. Other candidates could be such words as *effectiveness, efficiency, performance,* and *excellence*. Good positive words which conjure up essentially positive thoughts.

The three that are my personal finalists in the word-selection competition are essentially synonymous. They are *achievement, results,* and *success*. My winner, though, is the word success—success not just in resolving crises or meeting short-term challenges, but success in the fullest sense. Success implies the achievement of our goals and the fulfillment of our mission. And among our goals and within our mission statement would be process elements as well as content, working toward principled results.

Chapter 29

If You Believe in Teamwork . . .

I asked, "Why doesn't somebody do something?" Then I realized, I was somebody.

Unknown

What's past is prologue. So, here we are, ready to look to your future as a better teammate or more effective team leader.

Hopefully the first section has given you a chance to gain some new insights into the characteristics and natural causes of poor teamwork. Such insights should in themselves be helpful to you because, as has been said often, understanding the problem is at least half of the solution. Nevertheless, sections two and three should help you avoid having to re-invent the wheel as you undertake teamwork improvements.

You not only will be able to be a good team player, but you also should be in a position to help others walk down the teamwork path with you. And don't forget the importance of feedback! By keeping an open atmosphere and remaining approachable, you and others will be able to help each other stay on the teamwork track.

Although anyone who understands the nature and origin of teamwork challenges is in a prime position to prevent or resolve them, nothing else will be as important to your growth as a team player as the level of commitment you will make to foster your own improvement!

As was described in Chapter 8, the concept of "meeting you halfway" is as American as motherhood and apple pie. But your commitment to meet someone halfway would not be an absolute commitment to teamwork. It would be a conditional commitment. In essence, it would be a commitment to be only as good at teamwork as some other person. There is a risk—indeed a probability—that you would know how hard *you* would be working to be a good team player, but that you would not know how hard the other person may be working at it as well. Predictably, you or your teammate at some point would perceive the other as falling short of team-oriented conduct and the person perceiving himself or herself as going more than halfway would in turn slow down his or her teamwork efforts until the other catches up. The teamwork relationship would be in a downward spiral, and you and your associate would steadily return to your old individual—and sub-optimizing—ways.

So, if you wish to become an exemplary team player, I suggest you commit to teamwork absolutely. Don't let the deceptive "I'll meet you halfway" trap get in the way.

Similarly, don't let excuses get in your way as you press onward with your exemplary teamwork behavior. One can always find a potential cop out such as "I don't have time to seek advice or consider the needs or interest of others if I'm going to be a dynamic individual." Or you might rationalize by saying that teamwork isn't recognized and rewarded adequately by your boss, so why bother. You might even resign yourself to the idea that your organization's culture does not include a widespread pursuit of teamwork, and you might feel it therefore would be too difficult or frustrating for you to try to set a good example.

See how easy it is to blame someone or something else! How easy it is to excuse ourselves for not having communicated, or coordinated, or cooperated as well as we might have. How easy it is to say (and maybe even believe) that we are too busy. Yet we set our own priorities, and we decide what will keep us busy. Our actions are of our own instigation. Only we can prioritize and control our actions—and also our reactions!

People who are reluctant to take responsibility for their actions and reactions are likely to be heard making such comments as, "He makes me angry!" Yet one progressive school of thought holds that one person cannot make another angry. Instead, this school suggests that the person who gets angry does so himself or herself as a result of inadequate self-control. It is suggested, for example, that the person who presumably makes another angry does not have a bucket of "anger" with which to paint the other person. Indeed, the first person may do something which the second person doesn't like—but the reaction of the second person is strictly in his or her own hands.

Time goes on. The world continues to turn. And things continue to happen all around us—and *to* us. But it is up to each of us as to how we will act and react. It is up to us to take charge of our own destinies. It is up to us to determine our own values, our own priorities, our own strategies, our own actions, and our own reactions. And it is up to each of us to determine the extent to which we will communicate, coordinate, and cooperate with others at work, at home, or wherever we might be.

I urge you to accept the responsibility to become the superb team player that you know you could be if you made an *absolute* commitment to do so. Each of us can make a difference, but only if each of us commits to go for it—and then follows through without wavering. If each of us waits for the others to beautify their teamwork lawns before we pull our own non-teamwork weeds, no progress will occur.

"If it's going to be, it's up to me!"

You *can* help create peak performance teams. But it isn't enough to hope for teamwork. We must *believe* in it! We also must *advocate* it! And beyond believing in it and advocating it, we must work at it until we make it work!

Index

A

Accountability, 191–92
Achievement
    in family, 183–85
    opportunity for, 24
    path to, 45–46
    importance of, in
        teamwork, 158, 207
Agendas, team members with
    alternate or distracting,
    29–30
Alspach, Dan, 116
American management,
    versus Japanese
    management, 133, 147
Antagonists, 32–33
Aristotle, 137
Assessment of strengths and
    weaknesses, 60–61
Aurelius, Marcus, 75

B

Bernstein, Al, 190
Besant, Annie, 3
Blanchard, Kenneth, 201
Boetcker, William J. H., 196
Bryan, William Jennings, 166,
    191
Burke, Edmund, 190
Burns, Robert, 156
Business, applicability of
    teamwork to, 66–71, 126

C

Canham, Erwin D., 190
Carlson, Chester, 23
Carlzon, Jan, 145, 201
Carnegie, Andrew, 85
Cavasos, Lauro, 191
Challenges, team members as
    major, 37
Change, implementing, 63
Choosing sides, 17
Churchill, Winston, 184
Cicero, 197
Citizens, teamwork
    opportunities as,
    193–95, 197–200
Citizenship, quotes on,
    190–91
Coaching
    for conflict resolution,
    167–75
    constructive, 60
Co-involvement, justifying
    investment in, 131–35
Commitment, to teamwork,
    210–11
Committees, problems with,
    108. See also Meetings
Communication
    and co-involvement, 131
    with customers, 116, 117,
    118
    and feedback, 152, 153
    in family, 187

Communication, *continued*
importance of, to
teamwork, 4, 17, 19,
75–76
in meetings, 107, 108,
109–10
on peak performance
team, 139
on special teams, 127, 129
with vendors, 116, 117, 118
Complaints, importance of, to
teamwork, 17–18
Compromise, and teamwork,
49–50, 210
Conflict resolution, feedback
and coaching for,
167–73
Conflicts, importance of, to
teamwork, 17, 18
Consideration, importance of,
to teamwork, 17, 66, 73,
77, 120
Constructive conversation
catalysts, for giving and
receiving feedback,
164–66
Content, relationship to
process, 146, 205
Controls, relationship with
goals, 146, 205
Cooperation
and co-involvement, 131
with customers, 116, 117,
118
and feedback, 152, 153
importance of, to
teamwork, 4, 19, 76, 80
on peak performance
team, 139
on special teams, 127, 129
with vendors, 116, 117, 118

Coordination
and co-involvement, 131
with customers, 116, 117,
118
and feedback, 152, 153
importance of, to
teamwork, 4, 76
on peak performance
teams, 139
on special teams, 127, 129
with vendors, 116, 117,
118
Criticism, importance of, to
teamwork, 17–18
Customer relations, 120
Customers
as always right, 142, 145,
204
employee contact with,
119–23
feedback from, 144, 157
recognition of importance,
138, 141–42
as team members, 115–18
Customer-vendor relations,
116–18

Decision-makers
and the making and
avoiding of decisions, 34
in peak-performance
organizations, 39
team-oriented, 46
Decision-making
in family, 180–81
listening in, 120
loop in, 131
participative style in,
120–21, 134

Decision-making, *continued*
  on peak performance
    teams, 143, 146
  steps in, 206
  subordinate role in, 123
  and team orientation, 46,
    47, 212
Decisions
  makers-and avoiders-of,
    34–35
  make-versus-buy, 115–16
  making principled, 61–62
Dedication, 7
Dedicated suboptimizer
    syndrome, 17
Delegation, 99–104
  guidelines in, 105–106
  philosophical
    considerations of, 104
Differences
  resolving, 167–74
  among team members,
    27–39
Disney, Walt, 130
Domain issues, 17–18
Dominant forces, 36–37
Drucker, Peter, 129
Durant, Ariel, 177
Durant, Will, 177

E

Edison, Thomas, 21
Education, 120
Educational Testing Service,
    191
Effectiveness, importance of,
    in teamwork, 207
Efficiency, importance of, in
    teamwork, 207
Einstein, Albert, 119

Eisenhower, Dwight D., 190,
    197
Emerson, Ralph Waldo, 52,
    122
Employee-management
    relations, 120
Employees
  contact with customers,
    119–23
  hiring harmonious, 89–90
  importance of good, 85–89
  involvement of, 119–23
  promoting existing, 90–91
Empowering, 202
Entrepreneurs, 22–23
Estes, Craig, 186
Evaluation of, teamwork
    criteria for, 79–83
Excellence, importance of, in
    teamwork, 213
Exclusion, 96
Expectations, identifying, 57
Expedience, 41
  versus principle, 146, 205

F

Family, teamwork in, 177–85
Farnan, Jack, 116
Feedback, 38
  in business, 181–82
  for conflict resolution,
    173–79
  constructive conversation
    catalysts in, 165–66
  from customers, 144, 157
  in family, 186
  giving, 39, 154, 157–63
  importance of, 151–56, 215
  lateral, 144
  mutual, 144

Feedback, *continued*
    receiving, 138, 162–64,
        166
    and teamwork, 8, 143–45
    upside-down, 144
Feynman, Richard P., 156
Fitting In (Josefowitz and
        Gadon), 96
Ford, Henry, 23, 79
Francis, Clarence, 93
Franklin, Ben, 125
Functional organization,
        126–27

G

Gadon, Herman, 82, 96, 97
Galileo, 121
Gandhi, Mohandas, 194
Goal delineation, 143
Goals
    in feedback, 158
    knowing and
        understanding,
        138–40, 207
    and open communication,
        183
    purposeful, 140
    relationship with controls,
        146, 205
Goals/values/policies
        framework, 139
Goethe, 187
Golden Rule, 49–52
Group, filling key needs of,
        28–29
Guidelines, for good
        teamwork in sports,
        55–62
Guillotin, Joseph, 49

H

Hale, Edward E., 5
Harassment, 18
Hazing, 96
Hiring
    effective team players,
        85–91
    helpful hints on, 89–90
Holtz, Lou, 13
Honachick, Chick, 12–13

I

Illiteracy, 189, 191
Immovable objects, team
        members as, 36–37
Incorporation, 96
Individual ability and effort,
        19
Individual expedience, as
        challenge to teamwork,
        41–47
Individualism, 41
Induction
    of new members, 91, 93–98
    supervisors' guide for, 98
Input, seeking others', 143
Insulters, 32–33
Interaction
    in family, 183
    on peak performance
        teams, 145, 204
Interdepartmental teamwork,
        10, 132
Interdependence, importance
        of, in teamwork, 11–14
International peace, quotes
        on, 197
International relations,
        teamwork in, 195–96

Interpersonal relationships, ten commandments for good, 72–73
Intradepartmental team, 10

James, William, 121, 158
Japanese management, versus American management, 133, 147
John Paul II, 186
Johnson, Samuel, 24
Johnson, 201
Josefowitz, Natasha, 96, 97
Just-in-time (JIT) program, 117

Keller, Helen, 21
Kelley, S., 198
Kennedy, John F., 190, 197
Kent, Arthur, 186
Kettering, Charles F., 166, 199
Kroc, Ray, 85

Lamm, Richard, 193
Lao Tse, 156
Lateral feedback, 144
Lateral relationships, 100
Later teamwork, 10
Lawns and weeds analogy, of teamwork, 15–20
Law of communication, in organizations, ix, 51
Lead, Follow or Get Out of the Way (Lundy), 120, 206

Leadership
empowering, 202
impact of people on, 91
participative, 120–21, 132–35
Lincoln, Abe, 195, 197
Lindbergh, Charles, 23
Listening
and interpersonal relationships, 72
and leadership style, 120, 122, 212
Lombardi, Vince, 55
Long-term interests, 46
Lundy, Jim, 7, 156

MacArthur, Douglas, 21, 23
Make-versus-buy decisions, 115–16
Management by walking around, 68
Mann, Thomas, 107
Marquis, Don, 195
Marriage, quotes on, 186
Maslow, A. H., 157
Matrix organization, 128–30
Mayo, Charles H., 131
Medication, 171
Meetings
holding successful, 109–11
problems in, 108
as teamwork tool, 107–109
Meir, Golda, 197
Mill, John Stuart, 156
Mission statements, 39
Morale, role of delegation in improving, 99–104
Morris, George P., 65

N

Neglect, 17
Newcomers
  supervisors' guide for
    inducting, 98
  welcoming, 93–98
Niemoeller, Martin, 196

O

Objectives, knowing your,
  56–57, 203
Olhoeft, Wally, 13–14
"One-Minute Manager," 201
Open conflicts, 17
Organization
  flip-flop of structure in,
    203–204
  functional, 126–27
  matrix, 128–30
  project-based, 127–128
  size of, and teamwork, 22
Orincon Corporation, 116
Oversight, 17

P

Parallel-path compensation,
  130
Parenting, quotes on, 186
Participative style, of
  leadership, 120–21,
  132–35
Patton, George, 21, 23
Peak performance
  organizations,
  decision-makers in, 39
Peak performance teams
  and feedback, 151–56

interaction on, 145, 205
and mutual respect, 24
secrets to, 130, 137–47
Peale, Norman Vincent, 151
Peer feedback system, 8
Performance, importance of,
  to teamwork, 207
Peter Principle, 90–91
Peters, Tom, 119
Planning, 146
Plato, 199
Pope, Alexander, 115
Porter, Scott, 91
Position, understanding your,
  57–58
Power, 202
  flaunting of, 182
Practice, 58
Principle, versus expedience,
  146, 205
Process, relationship to
  content, 146, 205
Project-based organization,
  127–28
Project teams, 126–28, 130
Promotion, existing
  employees, 90–91
Prosperity, quotes on, 197

R

Reader's Digest, 191
Recognition, 158
Recruitment, of effective team
  members, 85–91, 122
Relationships
  in building teamwork, 45,
  50, 88
  ten commandments for
    good interpersonal,
    72–73

Results, importance of, in teamwork, 45, 207
Retaliation, 18–19
Rockefeller, John D., 85, 91
Role, knowing your, 57
Roosevelt, Franklin D., 197
Roosevelt, Theodore, 99, 190
Rules, knowing the, 57

S

Sabotage, 17, 18
Sangster, Margaret E., 186
Scandinavian Airlines, 145
Schooling, 120
Schweitzer, Albert, 190, 199
Selection, of team members, 85–91, 122
Self-discipline, maintaining, 58–59
Self-esteem, 73
Self-interest, 193–94
Self-respect, 121
Shakespeare, William, 156
Shaw, George Bernard, 195
Short run approach, to problem solving, 44–45
Sides, choosing, 17
Sikorsky, Igor, 23
Simpson, O. J., 13
Socrates, 156
Solzhenitsyn, Aleksandr, 197
Specialist, supervisor as, 10
Special teams, 125–30
Spirit dampeners, 35–36
Strengths, assessing, 60–61
Stress management, 99
Subordinates
    and coordination, 9
    contributions by, 121
    and decision-making, 123
and giving/receiving feedback, 143–45, 157–66, 177
and listening, 122
in organization structure, 203
and participative leadership, 132
recruitment of, as team members, 122–23
and review process, 133
Success, importance of, in teamwork, 46, 207
Superstars, as team members, 21–25, 42
Supervisors
    and decision-making, 123
    and giving/receiving feedback, 123, 143–45, 155, 157–66
    guide for inducting newcomers, 96–97, 98
    and listening, 120
    in organization structure, 203
    and participative leadership, 132
    and review process, 133
Supervisor-subordinate conversation guide, 158–59
Syrus, 166

T

Talent, getting and developing, 59
Talkers as team members, 31–32
Team leader, 5
    qualities of good, 25

Team members. *See also*
    Teamwork
  characteristics of poor,
    7–10
  customers as, 115–18
  differences in, 27–39
  with distracting agendas,
    29–30
  dominant forces and
    immovable objects,
    36–37
  and goals, 158
  helping less effective, 61
  identifying perfect, 39
  importance of being, 3
  insulters and antagonists
    as, 32–33
  interdependence of, 11–14
  major challenges in, 37
  makers-and avoiders-of
    decisions as, 34–35
  recruiting, 85–91, 122
  roles of
    alligator, 37
    big "I", 35
    bigot, 37
    cat-napper, 38
    civic-minded pillar, 29
    competitive actor, 31
    dark cloud, 35
    dedicated
      sub-optimizer, 31
    defensive tackler, 36
    dictator, 34
    flirt, 38
    guilty apologist, 29
    helpful reluctant, 29
    hero, 35
    iceberg, 35
    impartial observer, 28

    impatient fidgeter, 35
    impractical dreamer, 33
    jovial clown, 38
    juggler, 37
    know-it-all, 32
    mediator, 28
    motor mouth, 32
    moving freight train, 36
    nest guarder, 31
    note taker, 28
    orator, 31–32
    parade sweeper, 30
    passive follower, 28
    perfectionist, 33
    persistent pest, 32–33
    preacher, 32
    prime mover, 28
    primper, 38
    procrastinator, 34
    proverbial yes person,
      29
    quiet wizard, 33
    risk taker, 34
    rock of gibraltar, 36
    scatterbrain, 38
    spirited water spider, 38
    tattler, 32
    tender flower, 37
    trader, 36
    trail blazer, 28
    utility player, 28
  selecting, 85–91, 122
  spirit dampeners as, 35–36
  superstars as, 21–25
  talkers as, 31–32
  and team goals, 138–40
  with territorial interests, 31
  those who fill key needs
    of a group, 28–29
  under-appreciated, 30

Team members, *continued*
  unique but useful, 33–34
  useless baggage as, 38–39
  vendors as, 115–18
  welcoming new, 59–60,
    93–98
Teams
  intradepartmental, 10
  peak performance, 24,
    130, 137–47, 151, 205
  project, 126–28, 130
  special, 125–30
Team sports, observations
  about, 55–62
Teamwork. *See also* Team
  members
  basics of, 5, 137–47,
    201–207
  belief in, 209–11
  commitment to, 210–11
  compromise in, 49–50, 210
  criteria for evaluating,
    79–83
  delegation in, 99–104
  deterioration in, 17–20
  establishing and
    maintaining, 15–20, 44
  evaluating, 79–83
  in the family, 177–85
  and feedback, 8, 143–45
  Golden Rule in, 49–52
  guidelines for team sports,
    55–62
  and international relations,
    195–96
  levels in, 82–83
  meetings as tool in,
    107–109
  methods in, 65–71
  opportunities as citizens
    in, 187–89, 191–94

  pledge in, 47
  and size of organization,
    22–23
  truths in, 62–63
Territory issues, 17–18, 31
That's-not-my-job syndrome,
    18
Theresa, Mother, 186
They, 51
Tolstoy, 62
Total Customer Satisfaction
    (TCS), 201
Total Quality Management
    (TQM), 201
Truman, Harry S., 197
Twain, Mark, 196

Under-appreciated team
    members, 30
Understanding, importance
    of, in team members,
    207
Undesirable assignments
    stage, 96
Uniqueness, in team
    members, 33–34
Upside-down feedback, 144
Useless baggage, as team
    members, 38–39

Vance, Cyrus, 169
Vendors, as member of team,
    115–18
Volunteering, 4
  of ideas, 122

W

Walesa, Lech, 202
Walmart, 145
Walton, Sam, 145
Watches, gear analogy of
teamwork, 11–14, 42
Weaknesses, assessing, 60–61

Welcoming, of new
members, 93–98
We-they syndrome, 16,
127
What goes around comes
around, 49, 50, 52
Wooden, John, 13
Woolworth, F. W., 65

About the Author

Dr. Lundy has over 30 years experience in all levels of management, including the presidencies of two multimillion-dollar companies.

He established the recruiting, selecting, and training programs for a small business called The Haloid Company during the years of its most rapid growth. Shortly after he joined Haloid, the name was changed to Xerox. When he left Xerox he had risen to the presidency of its fastest growing division where sales and profits rose 400% in four years under his leadership.

Jim is currently president of Performance Systems, a management consulting company in La Jolla, California. Although his clients have included such giants as IBM, 3M, General Mills, TRW, Hewlett-Packard, General Dynamics, and American Express, his emphasis has been in assisting small organizations to grow and prosper.

Athletic scholarships, a Murphy Scholarship at Northwestern, and a Ford Foundation Fellowship at the University of Minnesota helped Dr. Lundy complete B.S. and M.S. degrees in engineering and a Ph.D. in business administration.

Jim's first book, *Effective Industrial Management* (1957) was adopted by more than a hundred colleges and universities and was also reprinted in India. His second book, *Lead, Follow, or Get Out of the Way* (1986), has been an American best-seller, and has been reprinted in England, Mexico, and China.

Jim Lundy's jam-packed publications and programs focus on key leadership and communication issues for optimizing individual and group performance. His emphasis is on communication, listening, involving others, teamwork, cooperation, interdepartmental collaboration, mutually agreed-upon objectives, tracking progress, and improving performance. In other words, achieving results!